Oklahoma City University
A Century of Service

Funding Provided by the Edith Gaylord Ethics in Journalism Foundation

*Oklahoma
Horizons Series*

Circa 1925

A Century of Service
Oklahoma City University

By Ryan McGee & Rebecca McFarland-Fenton

Managing Editor: Gini Moore Campbell
Oklahoma Heritage Association

Table of Contents...

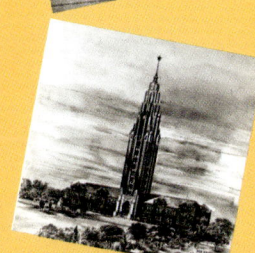

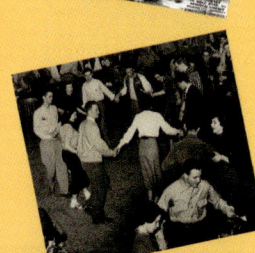

Special Thanks To:

For funding of this project, we would like to thank:
Ethics & Excellence in Journalism Foundation

To these and many more we are grateful for help with the research, resources, encouragement, and advice you gave throughout the production of this history book:

President Tom J. McDaniel, who had the foresight and faith to make this book a reality

Administrators who helped us through the writing and editing process, dedicating their time to ensure that the book adequately represents the university we serve:
Vice President for Student Affairs Dr. Richard Hall
Vice President for Institutional Advancement Art Cotton
Provost / Vice President for Academic Affairs Dr. Bernie Patterson
Vice President for University / Church Relations Rev. Leroy Thompson
Vice President for Administration and Finance Mary Coffey
Dr. Elizabeth Donnelly
Oklahoma City University Division of Student Affairs
Robert K. Erwin
Dr. Terry Phelps
Gini Moore Campbell, Managing Editor, Oklahoma Heritage Association
Bart Baker

Christina Wolf, the university archivist, who assisted us in research by gathering material for us, teaching us how to use the archives to find available resources, and sharing with us her vast knowledge about Oklahoma City University

Those who participated in interviews for the book, sharing their time and their memories

Dr. Brooke Hessler, who dedicated many of her students' talents to the production of different parts of this book and gave her own time and energy in helping with various stages of book production.

Those students who worked tirelessly to write captions for pictures:
Autumn Souders
Lauren Keller
Lauren Phelps Fitzgerald
Joanne Kurjan

Printed in the United States of America
ISBN 1-885596-39-1
Library of Congress Catalog Number 2004110529
Designed by Ryan McGee

Contributors:

Traci Ann Bair - A Super Man: Herbert Bagwell and His Musical Gypsies

Crystal Bell - Dr. Leona Mitchell: Grad Makes New York Metropolitan Opera

Cassie J. Bennett - Up in a Blaze of Glory: OCU Athletes Moon-Light as Firemen

A. Dunaway - A Family in Service: The Harrison Brothers Fight Together

Cassidy Logan Elms - Six Degrees of Beethoven: Dean Clarence A. Burg

Luke M. Elms - Cap 'n Kangaroo Court: The 'Frosh' Cap Phenomenon

Stephanie D. Joiner - Dynamite Diva: Kristin Chenoweth, Broadway Star

Scott P. Kedy - Presidents (timeline)

Gideon Keith-Stanley - A Call to Arms: The 344th Training Detachment

Sylvia Ann Kline - A Church Divided: The Lawsuit between the Methodist Churches

C. M. Mallory - Alice Conkling: Legendary Lecturer and Instructor

Dustin R. Murer - Pioneers Come in Pairs: Oklahoma City University Integrates

Eric Lee Peeples - Tradition and Community: Greek-Letter Organizations

Lyall C. Storandt - Teacher Gives Generously: Irminda Banning Bequeaths Estate to University

Jonathan L. Warren - Fight For Supremacy: Freshman and Sophomore Class Fight

Kali L. Watson - Sculpted to Sculptor: *The Eternal Challenge*

Matt Wills - Alvin Naifeh: Bringing Joy to Campus for More Than 50 Years

Jayroe

Foreword

The story of Oklahoma City University today and for the past hundred years is the story of students becoming the radiant stars that God created them to be. My story is not different from the others, just more noticeable than some.

It was the fall of 1964 and instead of being on a college campus close to my hometown with a full scholarship in tow, I was on the campus of Oklahoma City University as an incoming freshman. The walk from my mother's car to Walker Hall was emotionally a very long trip. But this was my dream. The size of the school, the location, the Methodist affiliation, and most of all, the reputation for excellence in music performance had always drawn me here. I would not be disappointed.

Inside my heart, there had been a secret while growing up in rural Oklahoma. I wanted to be a performing star. There was something about my soul that shouted to the heavens that I loved to sing on stage. I never thought success was likely. From my family environment, it would have appeared conceited to even share my dream with people outside the family, but the dream would not be denied. When I saw my first professional musical theater production, watched the Miss America pageant on television, or sang at countless weddings and school occasions, I could not ignore the incredible joy of performing and a calling to be more than I thought possible. I always knew that Oklahoma City University would be the right place to determine that future. Whether my future would be in the classroom—I majored in music education—or on a stage, this was the place for me to discover if my dreams were childhood fantasies or gifts from God.

From the tiny town of Laverne, with parents who were educators, I was able to attend this private university because of a partial scholarship, sacrificing parents, and a work-study program in the journalism department. It was the perfect choice for this small town girl with big dreams. Because I was shy and easily intimidated, I believe I would have gotten lost in a large university environment, but everything at Oklahoma City University fostered my growth in a positive way.

My experiences at Oklahoma City University led me to the Miss America Pageant and changed

my life in an incredible way. It wasn't that I was a star student at the university; I was not. During my freshman year in the music school I was double cast for the smallest part in the opera. I wasn't the best-prepared student for the rigors of Oklahoma City University's music school. I had very little music education in the small rural Oklahoma schools that I attended. Thanks to the world's greatest mother, Helene Grace, I had private voice lessons and piano lessons even if it meant that after a long day of teaching, she drove me to a neighboring town in order to have private instruction. Still, the music school was a challenge.

At that time the emphases at Oklahoma City University was classical music and opera. There was no musical theatre component. So, I was really out of my league in many ways. But like many other students, as long as I was willing to try, there were professors to help.

The music faculty always encouraged us even when we were struggling, especially when we were struggling. The leap of learning that was a part of the intense educational offering was inspirational. And it was not only in the music school that we received individual attention. It was just the way the university classes were taught—with each student in mind.

With the support of a caring faculty, advisors, and a nurturing network of loving friends, I summoned the courage to follow a dream and enter the Miss Oklahoma City Pageant. Actually, my sorority sisters pushed me into it.

My inner dreams of pageants and performances were no different than the hopes and desires of other students. We all wanted excellence in our lives whatever the field of study. That's the opportunity we received at Oklahoma City University. It was an incubator of aspirations, a nurturing boot camp, and a transition into adulthood. It was a university in the best sense, a place to learn, test your wings, and grow. It was this well-rounded education that helped prepare me for the variety of careers that I enjoyed: musical theater, sixteen years as a prime time television news anchor in Oklahoma City and Dallas, spokesperson for the Oklahoma Health Center and more recently Cabinet Secretary of Tourism for Oklahoma. The ability to be flexible in my career has a lot to do with a solid educational core.

The Oklahoma City University community was like a small town but with the advantages of a city…Oklahoma City, with its entertainment, shopping, and cultural opportunities. It was a university community that was filled with small groups that helped students have a strong sense of belonging. At the same time, it was also a well-integrated community. We all lived in the same environment, ate at the same place, and played together. We were not divided by sorority or major or interest. The divisions and different interests were just a part of the whole.

Since my graduation, I have watched the success of Oklahoma City University students from a distance and been proud. There have been some difficult days at the university, but still our students marched out into the world to make us all stand taller. Not only have our alumni gone on to medical school, Broadway, Miss America, prestigious boardrooms, courtrooms, art galleries, church pulpits, and political offices, but they can be found volunteering in the community, singing in the church choir, going on mission trips, and giving back in many ways to their communities. They are community builders and leaders who learned what true community is all about from a small private university on Twenty-Third Street in Oklahoma City.

As a trustee, for me this is the most exciting time in Oklahoma City University's history. Building on a tradition of faith, excellence, and service, we are stepping forward in grace and gratitude. With the generosity of the most incredible Oklahoma City University supporters, the University is building and filling facilities that are worthy of the best and the brightest.

Like the university, the Board of Trustees has survived changes and challenges. We have had incredible leadership in recent years from Herman Meinders and Bill Shdeed. They have been the examples for the rest of us to follow, giving their time, energy, financial resources, and hearts to Oklahoma City University.

The Scripture reminds us that, "where your treasure is, there your heart will be also" (Matthew 6:21). How blessed the university is to benefit from the investment by so many people of their "treasures" and their "hearts."

It's impressive that so many successful people in our community are willing to serve as Trustees. I think the reason is simple. It is rewarding to know you are making a positive difference in the lives of young people. It's fun to be part of a community of educational excellence. As Trustees, we consider it an honor to help build an institution that will live beyond our efforts and make a better world "one star at a time."

The star is a great symbol for our school not only because many of our students become outstanding in their fields but also because Oklahoma City University believes that each student is uniquely and Divinely created to reflect God's glory, like the stars in the heavens. We attract very special students. Our students are serious about their lives. They are purposeful. They want to develop their talents, live out of a sense of moral integrity, and develop a steady goodness that makes the world a better place.

Young people come to Oklahoma City University as rising stars. Here they find the support of outstanding faculty, a committed Board of Trustees, and admirable administration and great leadership in President Tom McDaniel and his wife, Brenda. This lays the groundwork for them to begin a stellar journey into significance as well as success.

Oklahoma City University is beginning to grow into its potential, as our city is starting its best time ever. The promise of this positive future is possible only because of the contributions of those who have gone before us. We all stand on the shoulders of those who have stood tall in the past. How important it is that we lay claim to our history with this book.

Before you begin your journey through these one hundred years of history, let us all take a moment to express gratitude for the lives that have been changed, the gifts that have been given, and the stars that reached their place in the heavens thanks to Oklahoma City University.

Jane Jayroe

Jane Jayroe

Jane Jayroe, Oklahoma City University's spokesperson for the centennial, as she appeared as a university co-ed in the 1960s

My association with Oklahoma City University began in 1968, as the United Methodist Bishop of Oklahoma, then as the Bishop-in-residence of the university, and ended in 1991 with the responsibility of teaching Biblical Literature to international students enrolled at the university. What I write is largely from memory because all of my records are in the Evangelical United Brethren Church and the United Methodist Church Archives. I am nearly ninety-four years of age. My memory is sometimes confused about dates and events; sometimes I don't even remember clearly.

I will begin by quoting the last paragraph I wrote in *The History of Oklahoma City University: A Miracle at Twenty-Third and Blackwelder.* "Oklahoma City University continues as a school of the United Methodist Church and Oklahoma City, in an institution dedicated to academic excellence on a campus where the spiritual dimensions of human life are recognized and their development encouraged." One of the reports of an early leader of the school said, "The meaning of life is service," and that is the special message of Oklahoma City University today – service to God and service to man.

I tried to imagine myself as one of the first students of Epworth University, the name of the school one-hundred years ago. It is September 7, 1904. I may have come from a small Methodist-Episcopal

Introduction

Bishop Paul W. Milhouse addressed graduates in 1971 during the commencement ceremony on the steps of the C. Q. Smith Student-Faculty Center.

congregation in a small town in Oklahoma, largely through the influence of the pastor's loyalty to the denominational project of a Methodist Church college in Oklahoma, and the conviction that I should begin my life's work with a college education. I may have worn knee-length trousers that buttoned at the knees, a cap, and perhaps a pullover sweater or a neatly pressed suit.

The college consisted of one building in a fifty-two acre field of weeds located at the top of a hill, and the power house that was under construction. Students arriving by the streetcar had to climb several wooden steps from the street to reach the field that was to become the campus, go north and follow the path made by farm wagons or by the cattlemen as they drove their herds across the plains. Not a tree was in sight.

A student said the building had a solid and firm appearance. It was built of white stone and red brick, with a small white porch in front supported with four white pillars. Another student said it gave one the impression of being alone and "confident of its strength to brave the World."

Faculty members met the students at the railroad station with white banners hastily printed with

Milhouse

the name of the university on them. They were shouting, "Right this way for Epworth University," and offering to help the students enroll. The students were met at the college building by members of the faculty, several board members, and some friends of the university. After devotional services were held, the students were classified, and regular classes began the next day. Enrollment was 116. It started out with the philosophy of being, "Christian without being sectarian," a philosophy to which it has faithfully adhered.

Those first years, like most church colleges, were spent in financial struggles and developing a student body. Within two years, Epworth's enrollment was more than 400. In a short time, schools of medicine, dentistry, pharmacy, law, and commerce were added to the existing academy and College of Liberal Arts.

The officials of the Methodist-Episcopal Church, South expressed their pleasure with the rapid growth of the university, but were unhappy with the fact that so many Methodist students were in other schools. A new faculty member called Oklahoma City "the most up-to-date twentieth century city in America…" Epworth University was closed in 1911, but there were people in the state who were determined to have a Methodist university in the State of Oklahoma, and the school reopened in the fall in the town of Guthrie, but closed again in 1919.

In the summer of 1919, Oklahoma City College opened for classes with a faculty of ten professors, with one serving as dean and one as a librarian. The first classes met in two remodeled apartment houses. On the front of the folder announcing the beginning of classes were these words: "We do not fairly judge a man by his clothes, nor people by their possessions. Oklahoma City College should not be judged by its temporary quarters…Out of our dwelling houses we have made a college center…We have changed butler's pantries into chemical laboratories, bedrooms became lecture halls… the space between the two houses…a chapel, and a gymnasium. The furnace room masquerades as a cafeteria…" The college was advertised as "distinctly a church school."

In 1922 Oklahoma City University had finally found a permanent home. Alumni from former colleges were transferred to Oklahoma City. Oklahoma City University has become one of the greatest universities of the United Methodist Church, the story of its development is preserved in the centennial book that follows. I am glad that I had the privilege of being closely associated with the school for twenty-three years of its life.

I worked closely with university officials in that time both as bishop of the Methodist Church and as the bishop-in-residence. I often ate in the faculty dining room with the professors and other leaders; I attended Chamber of Commerce meetings, listened to the lectures at the winter institute, and knew many of the civic leaders of the city that gave it birth.

I enjoyed teaching the international students Biblical Literature, and became familiar with their customs, holidays, and beliefs. Mary Frances and I attended their national festivals, had many of them in our home, took many to worship on Sunday, and visited museums with them in order that they might become better acquainted with the spirit of America. I can pay high tribute to them as giving evidence of sincerity in seeking an education, paying close attention to instruction, and being courteous in their relationships. Teaching them and becoming acquainted with them was a privilege of my retirement years.

During my last years of service as the United Methodist Bishop of Oklahoma, we almost lost the school. Enrollment was down. Finances were in bad shape, very difficult to get. The conferences and churches appeared to write the school off, and there were editorials in the newspaper that did us no good. I became aware of this situation shortly before conference time.

The agenda was fixed for the conference, but when we met for the annual session, I told the delegates that we would erase the agenda for Tuesday evening and devote all of the time to the university. The financial situation was fully explained. I told the delegates that at four o'clock the next afternoon they would be given an opportunity to place on the altar of the church a pledge card stating the amount they would contribute to the university during the next three years. I think that I stated a minimum figure to keep the school open. I said I had not come to Oklahoma to close the university.

The next day at four o'clock, we stopped all business, sang a hymn, and I gave the invitation. The aisles were soon jammed with people making their way to the altar of the church. Many had tears in their eyes. They came from the balcony and from every corner of the sanctuary, and laid on the altar their simple 3" X 5" cards that had been hurriedly mimeographed the night before. After the service the cards were counted. There was more than enough pledged that afternoon to keep the college open. A new attitude toward the college had developed overnight. Discouraged trustees were encouraged. A new president was called to the school. The university was saved!

Oklahoma City University is now one of the strongest universities of the church, with enrollment high and all departments strong. The foundation was laid for the great university that United Methodists have in Oklahoma today.

Paul W. Milhouse
United Methodist Bishop
Retired in 1980 from active service

It is an honor to be president of this university during an historic time. As we celebrate the first hundred years of Oklahoma City University, we look back at a century full of commitment to education and service, repeated affirmations of our strong support from the Methodist Church, and colorful men and women who lived our history. For example:

• So many pioneers blazed trails we follow to this day. President C.Q. Smith and his brother, Bishop W. Angie Smith, reached out to Native American tribes and opened international doors. Jerald Walker built on that foundation, encouraging Powwows on campus and Native American enrollment, and promoting creation of international programs that have made us a leader in business education around the world.

• Our Goldbugs football team also served as local firemen. Our freshmen once sported special caps to denote their rank, and were only too eager to burn them ceremoniously later in the year. We were the Thunderbirds for about two weeks in the mid-1940s before being dubbed Chiefs.

• Our students have performed all over the nation and the world, building a reputation for the performing arts that is unparalleled. Some of our brightest stars were in performance ensembles like the Surrey Singers that we still have today. Three Miss Americas and more than twenty Miss Oklahomas were students at our university.

- Our students have become great preachers and teachers, skilled doctors and nurses, leading scientists and lawyers, noted public servants and artists.

- The very first chapter of the (now national) biology honor society, Beta Beta Beta, was formed on our campus in the 1920s by Dr. Frank Brooks.

- Astronauts and film stars, opera luminaries and foreign dignitaries, bestselling authors and religious leaders, political and business giants – we have seen all kinds of distinguished guests visit our fair city and beautiful campus.

All of these things are just a taste of what you will read inside the covers of *A Century of Service*. The centennial book project was student-driven, and I am proud to be associated with an institution that encourages its students to follow their hearts and is supportive of the projects they wish to pursue to develop their talents.

We have successful alumni all over the world. This book gives some idea how much progress has been made in the first century of building a quality Methodist private university that nurtures tomorrow's leaders in service to their communities. We are proud of what has been accomplished and know our future is bright as we continue to light the world, one Star at a time.

Tom J. McDaniel
President

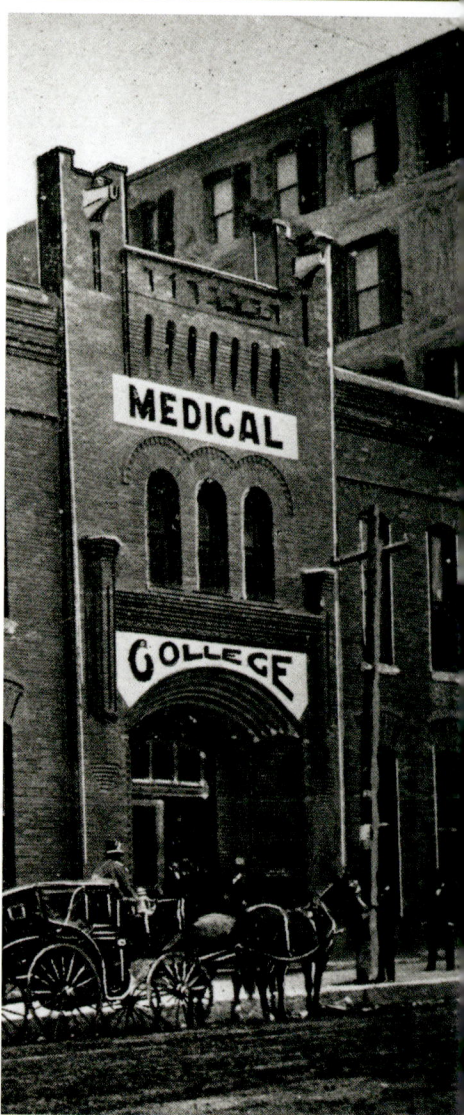

Territorial Triumph: Scenes from the trying days before statehood. Top row, from left: the first Protestant church in Oklahoma; an early group of Epworth University graduates. Middle row, from left: Judge C. B. Ames; a group of Epworth women with instruments; Fort Worth University's college of medicine. Bottom row, from left: the main building on the campus of Epworth University as it appeared in 1904; the first Methodist-Episcopal Church in Oklahoma Territory in Oklahoma City.

Rough Beginnings

Chapter One

1904

The early years of Methodist education in the south were filled with turmoil. Universities were opened and closed abruptly for many years, and the church struggled to financially support an institution of higher education on the prairie.

Texas Wesleyan University in Fort Worth, Texas, opened its doors in the fall of 1881. Its name was changed to Fort Worth University in 1889.

In Oklahoma Territory, The Methodist Episcopal Church, North, and the Methodist Episcopal Church, South, joined forces to support an institution similar to Fort Worth University. Classes began at Epworth University in Oklahoma Territory at 18th Street and Classen Boulevard in Oklahoma City in the fall of 1904.

Epworth University and Texas Wesleyan University grew quickly because of a demand for higher education, but both fell short in their ability to financially sustain necessary programming.

When Epworth University closed in the spring of 1911, the bond between the Methodist Episcopal Church, North, and the Methodist Episcopal Church, South, dissolved as well. Determined to have a church-affiliated institution of higher learning in Oklahoma, the Methodist Episcopal Church, North, created Oklahoma Methodist University. Like its predecessors, the university struggled with mounting debt. The school had a difficult time retaining students and finally closed its doors after the spring semester of 1919.

Right: Fort Worth University, Oklahoma City University's predecessor, stood on the Texas plains until its closure, in the late 1800s. Facing page: *The Lasso* yearbook staff of Fort Worth University worked to carefully record the institution's history.

Roots in Texas

From its beginning Oklahoma City University was a miracle, founded in the lawless days preceding statehood as the gunmen of the old west succumbed to the rigors of modern industry and the nation mourned the assassination of President William McKinley.[1] The excitement of the west began to wane as education fought to lay down roots on the frontier.

From its conception Oklahoma City University's foundation was in service; service not only to the university, but to the community and the nation. This pioneering spirit in both academics and service was certainly present when the Methodist-Episcopal Churches of Oklahoma and Texas ventured into the wilderness of higher education as they founded Texas Wesleyan College on June 6, 1881. The institution opened its doors in a temporary location the following fall. Five years later the college moved to its permanent home in south Fort Worth, Texas,[2] and a mere eight years later the college's charter was amended, changing the name to Fort Worth University.

In the institution's early days it received a telescope as a gift from H.B. Chamberlain, a native of Denver, Colorado, who donated the instrument after he decided to return to his home country, the United Kingdom. The telescope would remain a part of the university for many years and aid students in understanding the science of astronomy.[3] The telescope would follow faculty and students to two successive institutions of higher learning, ending at Oklahoma City College in the early 1920s.

On April 19, 1911, the Fort Worth University board of trustees met in St. Paul's Methodist-Episcopal Church of Ft. Worth, Texas, and dissolved the institution. One month later, the trustees met again to divide the net proceeds from the institution. The remaining monies primarily benefited three new colleges, one of which was Oklahoma Methodist University in Guthrie, Oklahoma.[4]

The Oklahoma Methodist-Episcopal Conference had been discussing involvement in higher education since the 1892 annual conference. The following committee report was given as the final item of business during the annual conference.

We recommend that the conference give early and energetic
attention to the matter of the establishment of two or
more good conference seminaries to furnish our young
people a good course of study of advanced grades. We also
recommend that a committee be appointed to confer with
any parties who may have propositions to make pertaining
to the location of any such school as the conference may
elect to establish.[5]

The Growth of Education in Oklahoma Territory

Less than one year after the Methodist-Episcopal annual conference decided to
embark upon an educational venture, the Legislative Assembly of Oklahoma Territory
enacted a law giving the Oklahoma Methodist-Episcopal Church its charter and named
a board of trustees.[6]

One month before Fort Worth University was formed, Anton Classen, a lawyer
from Chicago, Illinois, participated in the land run of 1889 into Oklahoma Territory.
Classen settled in Edmond, Oklahoma, and became editor of the local newspaper,
The Edmond Sun. Classen was a known advocate for higher education, and in the
early days helped to develop the Territorial Normal School in Edmond, later known
as the University of Central Oklahoma. This did not satisfy Classen's desire to
provide Christian education to the masses in Oklahoma Territory. As a member of
the Methodist-Episcopal church, he desired to form an institution that cultivated the
intellects of youth and fostered their spirituality.[7]

During the 1894 annual conference an attempt was made to establish Methodist
Hall at Territorial Normal School in Edmond. The proposition did not meet the board's
approval. A similar attempt to establish Oxford Hall in Norman, Oklahoma, also

A Church Divided
The Lawsuit between the Methodist Churches
Contributed By Sylvia Ann Kline

The Oklahoma Supreme Courtroom, filled with stone-faced lawyers and supporters from either side, was a scene of relief. What began fourteen years earlier as an agreement had become a case of land ownership between the Methodist Episcopal Church, South, and the University Development Company, employed by the Methodist Episcopal Church, North.

At a meeting of the board of trustees on January 3, 1911, the trustees recommended to the churches that the property be returned to University Development Company and that classes not continue beyond the first semester of the 1910-1911 year, unless the university could complete the academic year without incurring further indebtedness.[1] The school did in fact close in January, 1911, after the Methodist Episcopal Church, North, withdrew its support of the university and started another Methodist institution of higher learning, Oklahoma Methodist University, located in Guthrie.[2] The southern branch of the church still considered the university alive and put 21 southern Methodists on its board of trustees.[3]

Ruin was on the horizon and the Methodist-Episcopal Church, South, was slow to accept the university's fate. Afraid of losing the deed to the land because the school would close, the Southern Methodist-Episcopal Church asked the University Development Company to allow it to mortgage the university property. By allowing them to mortgage the property, the University Development Company would be held responsible for costs if Epworth did not pay the mortgage.[4] Epworth University had mortgaged its property to E. C. Thorne on July 16, 1910. The mortgage was made to State Life Insurance Company.[5]

By August 7, 1911, Epworth had made no payments on the mortgage, and State Life Insurance Company foreclosed on the mortgage. On August 13, 1913, the court awarded the State Life Insurance Company $40,700, yet did not decide if the lands were owned by the Methodist-Episcopal Church, South, or by the University Development Company.[6] This matter was not decided until September 24, 1917. The court ruled in favor of the University Development Company stating that the church had no right to university lands and that they would have to pay the now non-existent Epworth University $42,000.[7] Because of this ruling the church was forced to sell off some of the university lands to pay the mortgage back to the State Life Insurance Company.

Outraged by the court's decision, the University Development Company took the case to the Oklahoma Supreme Court. This time a compromise was reached. The church would own the ten acres known as campus land. All other land would be sold off at foreclosure prices to satisfy the judgment for the State Life Insurance Company and other outstanding debts. Any extra money would go to the University Development Company after paying all of the south church's attorney fees and court costs.

[1] Marion R. Baker, *Epworth University and Why it Failed: Methodist University and Why it Failed* (Oklahoma City: Oklahoma. OCU Box 103, University Archives and Special Collections), 11.

[2] Ibid., 12.

[3] Ibid., 14.

[4] *The South Methodist Church v. University Development Company*, Oklahoma Supreme Court, 1919 (Oklahoma City: Oklahoma, Box OCU 103, University Archives and Special Collections)

[5] Baker, *Epworth University and Why it Failed: Methodist University and Why it Failed*, 19.

[6] Ibid., 20.

[7] Ibid., 22.

Anton Classen played an important role in the formation of Epworth University.

failed. However, during this session of the annual conference the trustees of Oklahoma's first Methodist University were established.[8]

Joint Venture in Higher Education

In 1901 the two branches of the Methodist-Episcopal Church, the Methodist-Episcopal Church, North, and the Methodist-Episcopal Church, South, united to establish a university in Oklahoma City.

> In 1901 the commercial club of the city [Oklahoma City], through its president, Mr. Anton H. Classen, a leading member of the Methodist-Episcopal Church, and the honorary C. B. Ames, a leader in the Methodist-Episcopal Church, South, presented to the Indian Mission Conference and the Methodist-Episcopal Church conference a proposition looking to the founding of a university under joint ownership of the two churches.[9]

From the Methodist-Episcopal Church's establishment in Oklahoma Territory, education had been of great importance, and now both the north and south churches' dreams of forming a Methodist-Episcopal college were being realized. Copies of the official proposals were given to each conference in October, 1901. C. B. Ames presented the materials to the Indian Mission conference of the Methodist-Episcopal Church, South in Chickasha, and Classen delivered the findings to the Methodist-Episcopal Church, North in Shawnee.

Committees Were Formed and Plans Were Made

Eight months later, on June 22, 1902, at the United States Land Office in Oklahoma

Epworth University stood amidst the empty plains of Oklahoma Territory. The technologically-advanced university was equipped with a steam power house, electric lights, and running water.

City, three representatives from each branch of the Methodist-Episcopal Church and Anton Classen, president of the Oklahoma City Chamber of Commerce, met to discuss the actualization of the proposed university.[10] Although the southern conference voted unanimously for the proposition, the northern conference was met with "determined opposition" regarding the suggested location of the university. All opposition ceased, however, when the conference at Shawnee received word that the Methodist-Episcopal Church, South had already accepted the proposal.

During this same session of the annual conference, the bishop of each half of the Methodist-Episcopal Church appointed five laymen and five ministers to act as part of a joint commission to steer the formation of the new institution. The joint commission would be responsible for locating at least forty acres of land on which the university buildings would rest, and they were to secure $100,000 to support the school and its endowment. The joint commission agreed to meet and discuss the proposal in Oklahoma City on the first Tuesday of December.[11]

The joint commission's first meeting was held as planned in the parlor of the Third Street Methodist-Episcopal Church, South in Oklahoma City on December 3, 1901, at 3:00 p.m. During the evening session the chamber of commerce's proposal was adopted, and the joint commission gave birth to the University Development Company of Oklahoma City. Anton Classen was elected president and the commission adopted the name Epworth University.[12]

The City of Oklahoma City offered 240 acres of land with fifty-two acres set aside for the purpose of a campus at 18th Street and Classen Avenue. The remainder of the land was to be plotted as a town, and lots were to be sold. The proceeds from this endeavor would pay for the construction of an administration building and benefit the university endowment, classroom equipment, and other expenses.[13]

A President is Named and a University is Born

On April 24, 1904, the spring before the university was scheduled to open its doors, Professor R.B. McSwain of Southwestern University in Georgetown, Texas, was named as the new institution's president. McSwain long had been regaled as a scholar and assumed the position at the recommendation of Dr. W. McDowell and Dr. J. D. Hammons, the secretaries of education for the respective branches of the Methodist-Episcopal Church.

"It was not all sunshine that we encountered," Classen said prior to the school's opening in 1904. "There were some dark days. Some of my hearers will remember that in 1903, money was for a time scarce and could only be had at a price. Because of this, I had to borrow most of the money to finish our university building."[14]

Despite financial difficulty and other obstacles, Epworth University opened its doors as scheduled in September, 1904. The university included a college of liberal arts, a college of fine arts, and a preparatory school for high school students.[15]

Alice Conkling
Legendary Lecturer and Instructor
Contributed By C.M. Mallory

Imagine sitting in a small classroom listening to a lecturer who radiates with personality. She stands in front of wide-eyed college students giving romantic, yet accurate, accounts of the lives and works of Shakespeare and Chaucer. She demands silence from her students, but she rewards them with intoxicating lectures about the literature she loves. This woman was Alice Cowles Conkling.

Conkling received a Bachelor of Arts in British Literature from Oberlin College in Ohio, and became known for her grace and determination. After teaching many years at female seminaries in Illinois and California, she traveled to Fort Worth, Texas, and settled there to begin teaching. While there she taught at Fort Worth University.

This vivacious woman was able to transition from teaching affluent city girls to farm-raised boys. She was known for being partial to boys because of this and said once, "Because they have never known the truth of [English Literature and how to become a gentleman]."[1]

In the May 10, 1918, issue of *The Campus*, the graduating class "being of sound mind, lawful age and properly instructed" bequeathed to Conkling "a new device whereby absolute silence may be secured for ever and anon in the halls." Although the article did not specify what the device was, this incident implies Conkling's ability to be a personable teacher who appreciated inside jokes.

The Class of 1918 was not the only class that noted Conkling's personality and personal effort to provide a successful education. The graduating class of 1925 dedicated the 1924 *Scarab* annual to her with the words: "To Alice Cowles Conkling whose personality and character ever inspire in her students a determination to achieve that which is noble and enduring, do we the class of 1925 dedicate this volume."

Conkling often told her students awaiting a promising life, "Spend your life searching for jewels if you would find success."[2] This would be a motto she lived her life by. She followed the university to Oklahoma Methodist University in Guthrie and later to the campus at Northwest 23rd and Blackwelder, which eventually became Oklahoma City University.

Over the years, she taught English along with courses on British literature, especially courses on William Shakespeare and Geoffrey Chaucer. She was also a faculty advisor for the Sphinx Literary Society. The Sphinx was committed to the appreciation of literary creation.

On May 28, 1925, Conkling received an honorary Doctor of Letters from Oklahoma City University and became the first Professor Emeritus. This status provided her a $1,000 per year pension.[3] She went on to teach in the university's evening school and in the 1930s became the Dean of Women. During a 1936 committee meeting, she became the first woman honored as Dean Emeritus.[4]

Conkling will always be remembered by her students and those who surrounded her as a woman on a mission. As the editor of the *The Campus* stated in the April 6, 1926, edition, "Always a searcher for jewels, Miss Conkling has created the perfect jewel of lasting happiness—the service of an understanding friend." And this service was her distinct mark on the history of Oklahoma City University.

[1] "Miss Conkling Made Professor Emeritus after 34 Years Service," *The Campus*, 6 Apr. 1926, 2.

[2] "Miss Conkling Made Professor Emeritus after 34 Years Service." *The Campus* 6 Apr. 1926: 2.

[3] Milhouse, 61.

[4] 1925-1943 Oklahoma City University Catalogs, 1937.

The university building Classen had borrowed the money to build was completed at a cost of $40,000, half of which was pledged by the Oklahoma City Chamber of Commerce.[16] It stood three stories high and boasted all the amenities of a modern structure. The sandstone and brick façade housed electric lights, steam heaters, and the most up-to-date equipment available. The venture appeared to be a success and a marvel of modernity. The building eventually became Epworth United Methodist Church.

Shortly after construction of the campus' main building, a $6,000 powerhouse was built west of the university building. Just north of the university building, a two-story frame girls' hall was built with a large dining room and thirty-two rooms for residents. The last building to be erected at Epworth University in 1904 was a two-story brick building on the campus' northeast corner built by the federal government to house the United States Weather Bureau.

On September 10, 1904 the faculty assembled and prepared for the admission of students. Although faculty members were anxious to begin instruction, they had little luck finding housing when they arrived in Oklahoma City.[17]

> . . . [We] saw the sun rise on Oklahoma City for the first time on August 28, 1904. Like most new-comers, the first thing that we did was fall into the hands of the real estate firms, and almost an entire day was spent in looking for property either for sale or rent. Nothing suitable having been found we turned our attention to the list of homes which had been advertised with the University, the fact that they desired roomers and boarders, in hope of finding rooms and board near the new institution. Before we had made many calls, however, we decided that the prospective boarding

Oklahoma Methodist University was housed in the Oklahoma Territorial Capitol Building in Guthrie, Oklahoma. Although the institution was only open for a few years, it did serve as the Methodist instituion of higher learning during the first World War.

The prairie surrounding the campus of Fort Worth University was barren and treeless during the struggling institution's early days.

house-keepers desired students and not professors and their wives. The time was passing rapidly and nothing had been found. It was Saturday and a location must of necessity be secured before night. After going to one place about the third time, the good woman said that she would take us for one week, or until the next Saturday. The concession, of course, was great relief to us. . . We were "At Home" but with the understanding that it was to be only a week at a time.[18]

Only a few months after Epworth University welcomed new students and faculty to the campus, President McSwain suffered a nervous breakdown, brought on by the pressures of financial turmoil of opening a new university. Following his breakdown, McSwain resigned from office, and his term as president was completed by Professor G. C. Jones of the university's chemistry department. The following summer, George H. Bradford assumed the roll of university chancellor, and Jones continued as vice chancellor.

Rapid Growth Stunts Progress

On September 11, 1904, 175 students filled the main university building's chapel for Epworth's opening sessions. By the fall of 1907, enrollment had increased to 400 students. As the number of students increased, Epworth's needs began to change. During the 1907-1908 school term, lab facilities and a library were added to campus. In addition to new facilities on the campus, Epworth University was growing across the city. In only three years the university had acquired a commercial school, a law school, a pharmacy school, a school of dentistry, and Oklahoma's first school of medicine.[19]

The school of medicine was established with donations from twenty-one doctors and surgeons, each of whom gave $1,000 for the purchase of the Angelo Hotel and the necessary equipment for instruction. The new school was founded on the corner of Northwest 6th Street and Broadway Avenue in Oklahoma City. The Epworth College of Medicine remained self-supporting until it merged with the University of Oklahoma's already existing pre-med program. The University of Oklahoma assumed the responsibility of continuing education in the field of medicine and moved the institution to a new building at Northwest 4th Street and Stiles Avenue.[20]

1907 proved to be an eventful year for the young university. Besides the university's expansion into the fields of law and medicine, *The Campus*, Epworth's first yearbook, was published. Since no form of documentation had been maintained in the early days of the institution, the book chronicled the happenings at the university between 1904 and 1907. The book was renamed *The Wind-Up* in 1908, and finally the *Epworthian* in 1909.[21]

Although Epworth University seemed to be a success, it had grown at such a rapid pace that by 1911 the university was experiencing financial pain brought on by revenues too low to support the expansive academic programs. On January 3, 1911, an emergency session of the board of trustees was held to discuss the financial condition of the university. At 1:30 p.m. in the University Chapel, the fate of Epworth University was sealed with a unanimous vote by the board of trustees. The property on which the university sat and the surrounding land was to be returned to the University Development Company.[22] The university was to close its doors at the end of the semester.[23]

The Ides of March

A seemingly simple decision resulted in far-reaching ramifications. On March 17, 1911, the Methodist-Episcopal Church, North, through the process of church law, withdrew from the union controlling Epworth University. Upon the withdrawal of the Methodist-Episcopal Church, North the Methodist-Episcopal Church, South insisted the partnership could not be dissolved without the consent of both parties. The Methodist-Episcopal Church, South sued the University Development Company for its share of interest in the institution. After a myriad of conferences and legal proceedings, a compromise was reached. The Methodist-Episcopal Church, South received eleven acres of property and the university's main building, which became Epworth Methodist Church, and the property was developed into Classen High School.[24]

Also on March 17, the Oklahoma Methodist-Episcopal Conference met in Guthrie and determined that the remaining $31,000 cleared from Fort Worth University and Epworth University would benefit the construction of yet another institution. The merger between Fort Worth and Epworth universities formed Oklahoma Methodist University in Guthrie.[25]

This third attempt at instituting higher learning in what was now the State of Oklahoma was blessed by the state's University Senate on January 9, 1912; classes began meeting in Guthrie at the Territorial Capitol Building.[26] Oklahoma Methodist University was controlled solely by the Methodist-Episcopal Church, North, without any aid from the Methodist-Episcopal Church, South. The university was created under a charter granted by the Oklahoma State Legislature at the request of the Oklahoma Methodist-Episcopal Annual Conference.[27]

War Interrupts Progress and Stability

With the progress of the new university, Dr. Edward Hislop began a $75 million "centenary" campaign to raise money for the institution. However, his plans for expansion were interrupted by a war that was supposed to end all wars.

With the onset of World War I and few prospects for Oklahoma Methodist University to establish a permanent home, its enrollment dropped dramatically. Dr. Hislop summarized these woes to the board of trustees during his 1917 annual report.

> ...there has been no permanency of stability to the institution, so that young people have not in great numbers cared to risk their education with us. Endowments could not be secured, gifts for improvements, such as library and equipment, were impossible to get, having no permanent abiding place.[28]

Oklahoma Methodist University closed the 1916-1917 fiscal year with a $4,000 deficit and little promise for the institution's future.

Another Resurrection

Only one year later, and less than one decade of educational service, Oklahoma Methodist University closed its doors on June 14, 1919. Once again, the university's remaining assets were transferred to another new institution upon the payment of all outstanding debt.

During the Annual Conference of 1918, Bishop William O. Shepard developed an aggressive location committee. By March of that same year the committee had located and purchased 22 acres in Oklahoma City as the future home of Oklahoma City College. Oklahoma Methodist University would relocate to the city of its predecessor and assume a new name. The projected date for the fourth institution to open was September, 1919.[29]

Roaring through the twenties: Top row, from left: Students enjoy time on the beach; Charles Lindbergh breaks ground on the College of Fine Arts. Middle row, from left: Tri-Beta students head out to investigate wildlife; an aerial shot of the campus depicts the university grounds in the fledgling stage at the 23rd and Blackwelder location. Bottom row: the university seal, officially adopted in 1920 reflects the acceptace of graduates beginning in 1904.

Chapter Two

The
Golden
Age

1920

After the spring of 1919, Oklahoma Methodist University relocated to 12th Street and Walnut in Oklahoma City and began educating students under the name Oklahoma City College. Some of the faculty and staff of Oklahoma City College had followed Methodist higher education from Fort Worth University, Epworth University, or Oklahoma Methodist University to Oklahoma City College. Likewise, Oklahoma City College received assets from the predecessor universities. In spite of financial difficulties in its first few years, Oklahoma City College survived and maintained strong ties to the Methodist Church and the Oklahoma City Community.

In 1921, Oklahoma City College welcomed a growing enrollment. Athletics grew slowly and steadily throughout the institution's first few years, and in 1921, the Goldbug was established as the institution's first mascot. On December 5, 1922, Oklahoma City College's first new building was completed at Northwest 24th Street and Blackwelder Avenue.

In 1924, the institution's name was officially changed to Oklahoma City University. The board of trustees also voted to accept as alumni individuals who graduated from any of the university's predecessors, and the university seal was changed to reflect a 1904 date of establishment. With a new name and expanded list of alumni, the university forged ahead, adding programs and building campus traditions.

The north and south halves of the Methodist Episcopal Church in Oklahoma reunited in 1925, ending a feud that began with the close of Epworth in 1911.

The Golden Age

In the fall of 1919, as Oklahoma Methodist University again made a major move, this time back to the state's capital, there was no way of knowing if the waning institution would ever develop to its full potential. "The college year of 1919-1920 opened in confusion and uncertainty," stated President Green in his annual report to the meeting of the board of trustees in the spring of 1920.[1]

With a board of trustees forty-one strong, made up of two-thirds United Methodist clergy, Oklahoma City College was organized. Within six months the college opened its doors at a temporary location on the corner of 12th Street and Walnut, near downtown Oklahoma City, with a total budget of $40,000.[2] The temporary home consisted of two houses adjoined to construct a space for classrooms and a cafeteria.

It wasn't until March 17, 1920, that the $31,106.92 proceeds from the sale of Fort Worth University were finally forwarded to the university. It had been required that these monies not be received until the institution had a permanent home.[3]

Shortly after receiving these funds, the first ever commencement week was held. The events began with a chapel service at 10:00 a.m. on May 26, 1920. On May 29 a breakfast with the president was held. The following Sunday, baccalaureate was held at First United Methodist Church of Oklahoma City downtown, where Reverend I. Frank Roach, D. D., spoke to the students. A fine arts recital and a faculty reception were the final events leading up to the June 3rd commencement. Commencement ceremonies were held at 8:15 p.m. at the same location.[4]

On Statehood Day, November 16, 1920, the school for religious training opened with a mission to groom religious leaders of the future for the capital city.[5]

Oklahoma City College maintained other strong ties to the Methodist community. April 10, 1921, was named "Launching Sunday," beginning a campaign to ask Methodist congregations statewide for funding for the new institution. On Methodist pulpits across the city hung a banner reading, "This is our college, it is our opportunity, the time is at hand." Over the next five days Oklahoma City College raised $401,250 in additional funding toward the establishment of a new permanent home.[6] Before May of that same year Oklahoma City College had passed the half-million dollar mark. To raise all the necessary funds for the new campus by the June 8th deadline, $27,000 had to be raised daily to reach the million dollar goal.[7]

On Wednesday, June 8, 1921, closing day of the financial campaign, the campaign committee and the board of trustees met at noon and remained in session until that evening. At midnight, as the campaign drew to its official close, students from the university assembled on the northwest hill of the campus to show their rallying support for the hard work done by the administration in the preceding months.[8] In spite of the board and administration's diligence, they fell short.

In 1921 track made its debut on the Oklahoma City College campus. The first meet was held in Norman that April.[9]

In the fall of 1921 enrollment reached 250. Although the institution was still struggling to begin construction on its new home, the number of students attending classes climbed steadily.[10] The unanimous induction of Oklahoma City College's athletic programs into the Inter-Collegiate

Oklahoma City College was located in a temporary location at 12th Street and Walnut Avenue until the university completed the administration building in 1922.

Conference on December 10, 1921, was a sign that the school was growing at a faster rate than many had expected. Members of athletic teams were thereafter required to carry at least twelve hours of course work and earn passing grades in two-thirds of their classes.[11] That same winter Oklahoma City College formed its first wrestling team.[12] Earlier in the school year the athletic organization had been named the Goldbugs by President Green and *The Daily Oklahoman*.[13] The Goldbug was identified as the school's mascot because it was a "symbol of resurrection and continuing life."[14] It seemed an appropriate signifier for an institution with a rocky history of closure and rebirth.

On March 23, 1922, the entire student body boarded trolleys at 12th Street and Walnut Avenue to travel to groundbreaking ceremonies for the university's new location. The first spade of dirt was turned by Dr. I. F. Roach, pastor of First United Methodist Church of Oklahoma City.[15]

On December 5, 1922, the college's first new building was completed at Northwest 24th Street and Blackwelder Avenue.[16] Built in the English collegiate gothic style, the new edifice was intended to act for all posterity as a gateway to knowledge and to the university campus. The structure was meant to hold 600 students and house all the major functions of the institution except athletics. The tower at the center of the administration hall was used as

Cap 'n Kangaroo Court
The 'Frosh' Cap Phenomenon

Contributed By Luke M. Elms

The stern judgment comes down from the court. The accused gasps as the sentence is read—a sentence for a stunt so severe that if you are caught it may be the end of dignity as you know it. In the Kangaroo Courtroom a freshman reaps the consequences of disobeying a tradition that some considered hazing but others considered law—the freshman boy's mandatory skull cap or freshman girl's colors. The young girl tediously serves her sentence. One mouthful of water at a time she sucks the water up through the straw and blows it into the other cup. She got one cup. Others may have gotten worse.

Freshmen boys were required to wear a hat which was referred to as the freshman cap, frosh cap, or beanie. The cap was usually a felt beanie[1] that is described as a skull cap in the December 20, 1922, issue of *The Campus*. Freshman girls were not required to wear the cap "Because the cap does not fit a girl's head so well and musses the hair."[2] The caps were required for all times on campus or at any campus event. These rules were in place until the end of the year when the freshmen were allowed to burn the caps as a symbol of moving on to the sophomore year.[3]

A group called "The Enforcers" consisting of Bob Van House, Jimmy Baker, and Bill Lunsford carried away many rebel freshmen who were caught uncapped.[4]

According to Erwin Elms, 1971 Bachelor of Music, by that time "All of the freshmen were required to buy the cap, but none of us ever wore them."[5] And that is how the freshman cap tradition ceased to exist. One can only guess when the tradition finally faded into oblivion. However, one thing can be certain: throughout the tradition's years many bizarre sentences were inflicted on many nervous frosh.

This was just a typical day in the Kangaroo Court. The Kangaroo Court was a group of upperclassman that dealt justice on disobeying freshmen. While the punishment may not have been life changing, the tradition was real. The tradition that was in place from the early to mid-1900s later faded from Oklahoma City University's campus.

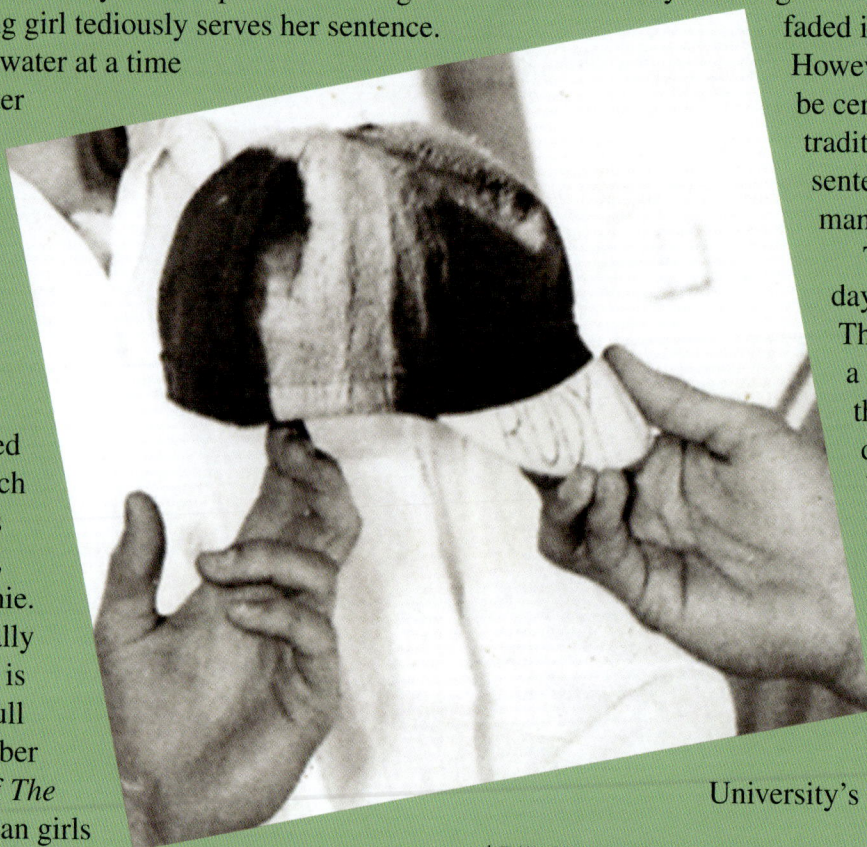

[1] Bill O'Neil, Panola County Texas Research Center, 17 Oct. 2003 and 05 Feb. 2004 <http://www.carthagetexas.com/Center/memories/freddy.htm>.

[2] "Frosh Doff Beanies, but Not to Sophs!" *The Campus,* 16 Oct. 1952, 1.

[3] Elms, Erwin, personal interview, 30 Jan. 2004.

[4] "For Yearlings Only," *The Campus*, 20 Dec. 1922.

[5] Elms, 30 Jan. 2004.

the library and stack room. [17]

University athletics grew to become a more important part of the campus community. During the 1922-1923 school year Oklahoma City College began to build basketball, track, and tennis teams.[18]

In January, 1922, Mr. and Mrs. R. E. Rice of Yukon proposed the purchase of lots near the new campus for the construction of a men's dormitory. The building was to be ready for habitation by the time the university transferred from Walnut Street to the permanent campus home at Northwest 23rd Street and Blackwelder Avenue. The Rices were the parents of 1925 graduate Paul Rice. [19]

In fall of 1922 the first courses in business administration were offered by the university. At the request of the Oklahoma City Chamber of Commerce, President Green formed courses for future Oklahoma City executives.[20]

In addition to new courses offered in business, a fraternal honors society was formed in the fall of 1922 by Professor Frank G. Brooks. The organization was established to honor students who excelled in biology. Over time the organization spread across the state, the nation, and eventually the world. Oklahoma City

Members of the Beta Beta Beta honors society spent time each year at Red Rock Canyon doing field experiments and learning more about the natural sciences.

College's chapter of Beta Beta Beta held the first charter ever issued to that national organization. Each spring, members of Beta Beta Beta attended a weeklong field trip to Falls Creek Campground in order to better study natural scientific phenomena.[21]

Eugene Antrim succeeded President Green as university president and was officially inaugurated on December 4, 1923, as a part of a three-day program.[22] Along with prominent educators from around the country, Oklahoma ministers celebrated the passing of the torch, ushering Oklahoma City College into its golden age.[23] Antrim believed the university must hold clear Christian principles.

> [OCC] Must offer courses in Bible, Religious education, ethics and Philosophy, which will conspire together to produce the highest type of Christian citizenship and train youth for ministerial, missionary, and civic leadership of distinctly Christian character anywhere in the World.[24]

After Antrim's inauguration, the number of faculty increased and more advanced equipment was purchased. Sixteen acres of land was bought directly north of the campus for the purpose of building a gymnasium, athletics stadium, and fine arts college.[25]

In October, 1923 the board of trustees adopted a university seal. The seal read, "Oklahoma City College, established 1919."[26]

The university appeared to be more successful than ever, as enrollment increased. The institution's deficit grew to $100 per student,[27] and only $432,000 of the $1.5 million promised during the Great Campaign of 1920 had actually been collected. More than two-thirds of the amount pledged was outstanding.[28] In October, 1924, enrollment reached an all-time high of 1,230 students studying on the newly built campus. The Walnut Avenue property had been remodeled as apartments and was now being rented out by the university.[29] During the 1924-1925 school year, two houses were purchased at the corner of Northwest 24th Street and Blackwelder Avenue to house the newly-founded College of Fine Arts. Finally, a grandstand with seating for 1,000 people was constructed on the campus.[30]

As many new buildings and structures were erected on campus, the street fronting the university was finally paved. As a way to show their appreciation to the institution, several male students planted grass and shrubs along the main thoroughfare.[31]

A Final Name Change
In 1924 the board of trustees voted to change Oklahoma City College's name

to Oklahoma City University. They also voted to recognize as alumni all individuals who graduated from any of the previous institutions that transferred assets to the university. With this vote the old name was legally nullified and the list of alumni grew.[32]

1924 proved to be a prosperous year for Oklahoma City University. Proud of its new status as a university, the institution established its first correspondence program in January. Students were required to produce nine assignments and take a final to gain class credit. The cost per credit hour was $4.58.[33] In addition to the newly initiated correspondence program, the university purchased its first printing plant in April. Rev. H. E. Brill, a former newspaperman and minister in the Methodist Church, was elected to manage the press in September. The press was installed in the basement of the Administration Building and readied for production.[34] In June of that same year Oklahoma City University's seal was redesigned to incorporate the new name and to reflect the date of establishment as 1904.[35]

The light in the Administration Building's tower was added during the 1924-25 school term. The tower was lighted in years to come following the victories of athletics teams.[36] In addition to this tradition, driven by school spirit, the university's first fight song was composed. Geraldine Patton, a member of the class of 1926, wrote the melody and words to the song "White and Gold." The song was chosen when the Yellow Jackets, the men's pep organization, conducted a songwriting contest.[37]

The administration building stood virtually alone when it was completed in 1922. A few Model T Fords sat parked in front of the university's only building.

Fight for Supremacy
Freshman and Sophomore Class Fight

Contributed By Jonathan L. Warren

It was a dark night, but they had all gathered around their fearless captain in anticipation. Suddenly the eerie silence broke as their captain yelled, "On your toes freshman; there is something in the air!"[1]

Nothing happened as they continued to search the dark shadows of the campus. Then a mysterious whisper spread throughout their side, "On your toes freshman, there is something in the air." The freshmen side was all ablaze as they spotted their first sophomore of the night.[2]

They all took off after this lone sophomore to protect their side from the dreadful enemy. They soon caught up with him and handcuffed him to a nearby pole. Not quite satisfied with just cuffing him to a pole, one of the other freshmen decided to cuff him to a nearby car. Unfortunately, the car had a file in it and the sophomore was able to escape.[3]

The rest of the night was uneventful as the freshmen waited for the sophomores to make their move. Just as they were about to give up on an attack by the sophomores, around came a car filled with them. Three freshmen took off after the sophomore class president, but were unable to tell where he had gone. Eventually, he was spotted trying to make his way up a tree where the freshmen had hung their class colors. Six freshmen grabbed hold of him, but it was too late and the sophomores unfastened the freshmen class colors and put up a sophomore class color. The freshmen had the last laugh though as one of them climbed up the tree, removed the sophomore class colors, and declared the freshmen class victorious.[4]

In the early years of Oklahoma City University, this scene took place every year as the freshmen and sophomores battled it out for supremacy of the lowerclassmen. For one entire day, members of these two classes went head to head in an all-out struggle against each other. The original goal was to see which could display its class colors more predominantly across campus. In the later years of the class fight, the winner was determined by several different events, including basketball, tug-of-war, a relay race, a plank pushing contest, a sack tying contest, and other smaller events. Each event was scored and the class with the most points at the end won the class fight.[5] Over the years the fight eventually evolved into a more organized set of competitions, but the goal remained the same—Beat the other class at all cost.

The class fight originated in 1911. Originally designed for males only, the fight became all inclusive as they admitted females in 1920. Little is known about the outcome of the earlier class fights, but during the twenties, *The Campus* picked up coverage of the fight. In 1921 and 1922, the sophomores were greatly outnumbered by the freshmen and lost the class fight.[6] In 1923, the sophomores again took a beating from the lowerclassmen.[8] In 1924, the sophomores regained some dignity as they tied the freshmen for the first time.[9] By 1925, it was back to normal as the freshmen regained their supremacy.[10]

[1] Gladys G. Gillette, ed., "Found- a letter," *The Campus*, 1 April 1921, 3.

[2] Gladys, "Found- a letter," 3.

[3] Ibid.

[4] Ibid.

[5] Lee Robinson, ed., "Underclassmen Tie in Class Fight," *The Campus*, 3 Oct.1924, 1.

[6] Gladys, "Found- a letter," 1.

[7] Alwyn Flemming, ed., "Freshman colors hoisted," *The Campus*, 3 April 1922, 1.

[8] Alwyn Flemming, ed., "Freshman Win Class Fight" Ibid., 5 April 1923, 1.

[9] Lee Robinson, ed., "Underclassmen Tie in Class Fight," Ibid., 3 Oct. 1924, 1.

[10] G. Lemuel Fenn, ed., "Frosh Vanquish Sophs in Annual Class Fray," Ibid., 2 Nov. 1925, 1.

In the fall of 1925 Oklahoma City University developed its first part-time school for working adults wishing to further their education. Classes met at Central High School in downtown Oklahoma City on Tuesday and Thursday evenings between 4:30 p.m. and 10:30 p.m.[38] Enrollment for the evening college's first year was 305, just more than half of the university's full-time enrollment.[39]

The 1925-26 school year was termed a "pioneer year in athletics." Ten new sports were added, including varsity basketball, tennis, golf, hockey, archery, volleyball, handball, and recreational hiking. With these expansions two clay tennis courts and a nine-hole golf course were added.[40]

As one of the many additions to the intramural program, archery instruction began in 1925 under the instruction of Dean of Intramurals, R. L. Grismer. Grismer, formerly of Oxford University in the United Kingdom, instructed the Permian Red in the finer points of the sport. Archery classes were available only to women wishing to exercise their athletic skills.[41] While some women enjoyed the art of casting arrows, others spent time on the basketball court.

During the 1925 season the Gold Middies emerged as a vital part of university athletics. They played a schedule of fourteen games, losing nine. In spite of their less than successful first season, the Gold Middies had established themselves as a force in women's athletics across the state.[42] The Gold Middies' second season was much improved over their first, although they were forced to play several high school teams due to a lack of women's athletics in the area. They did, however, win two important games, one against Oklahoma Presbyterian College and the other against Oklahoma Baptist University.

During the fall football season Coach Lynn O. Waldorf had twelve returning lettermen,

The Pepettes, the university's first organization with open membership, cheered for the Goldbugs during athletic events as well as offering social opportunities for the young ladies of the university.

Throughout the university's history, the Goldbug Gymnsium was used not only as a gymnasium, but as a library, and eventually a student dining room. Many former students of the university remember the Goldbug fondly.

most of whom were linemen.[43] Oklahoma City University broke into the winning column in the conference, winning three conference games.[44]

Oklahoma City University finished second, with twenty-six points, in the Annual State Track and Field competition. The May 24, 1926, edition of *The Campus* called the win "…the biggest surprise of the season." During the meet, Ed Doyle set a state record in the javelin throw after launching the spear 162 feet and ten inches. The Goldbugs placed in every event but the broad jump and the mile.[45]

As athletics became more prominent on campus, new forms of campus employment cropped-up as well. Agriculture became a practical method of making money for OCU students in 1925. Cotton was planted on fourteen acres at the campus' northwest corner. President Antrim believed this new endeavor was a way not only to conserve land that had been added to the campus, but to establish employment for those willing to pick the cotton when it was ready.[46] Once the cotton was harvested and ready for sale, the Disciples of Christ purchased the full harvest. They gave the bolls of cotton to 10,000 people at their annual national convention as tokens of their participation in the event. The bolls were dyed different colors intended to show the rest of the nation the "fruits of Oklahoma."[47]

As the university grew academically, it became necessary to expand physically. On March 24, 1925, the university purchased twenty acres of land from Furr and Company for $30,000. The land stretched from Florida Avenue to Indiana Avenue between Northwest 25th Street and Northwest 27th Street.[48] The purchase of land for expansion came none too soon. By 1926 enrollment reached another significant peak at 1,500.[49]

The university had few traditions in its early days. With the founding of the university's Student Council, tradition began to arise. One of the first decisions made by the newly-formed council was the institution of the freshman cap, a tradition already held by many Ivy League institutions. All freshmen were required to wear green caps to signify their classification and to build community and school spirit.[50] The caps, typically abhorred by freshmen, were traditionally worn through the first semester and then burned at a bonfire following the Thanksgiving football game.[51]

Construction of a gymnasium, the Goldbug Gym, was completed at a cost of $22,000.[52] The Goldbugs played their first game in the new facility against the University Preparatory School Mavericks on Friday, December 18, 1925.[53] The Goldbug Gym seated almost 500 people.[54] Athletic Department Chairman George Fredrickson managed the facility.[55] The facility also served as an armory for the Oklahoma City University division of the National Guard.[56] Although the gym was originally intended to be constructed of sheet metal, the plan was abandoned early in the school term and revised to match the gothic style of other buildings on campus.[57]

A $1.5 million campaign was launched in February, 1926 to increase the university's endowment and construct several new buildings.[58] The campaign was divided into three separate target areas: the campus (faculty and staff), the Oklahoma City metropolitan area, and the State of Oklahoma.[59] The university's students set a campaign goal to raise $70,000 among themselves, and by March, 1926 they had raised nearly half that amount with $33,000 in hand.[60]

During President Antrim's administration the two feuding halves of the Methodist Church reconciled their differences and reunited. On December 21, 1925, the two bodies formed a Joint Commission for the Reunification of the Methodist Church. On March 10, 1926, the commission reported that the Methodist–Episcopal Church, South, would raise a total $300,000 and $200,000 in security,[61] $50,000 of which secured their share of the property. The commission's proposal was approved unanimously, and it was agreed the money would be raised over a five-year period.[62] A program of unification was held on Oklahoma City University's campus to commemorate the merger.[63] As the university grew, its financial situation worsened. Members of the faculty, administration, and staff helped alleviate the budgetary stress, as they were required to contribute five percent of their salaries each month to the university.[64]

Colonel Charles Lindbergh, who made the first transatlantic flight, turned the first spade of dirt at the groundbreaking for the new Fine Arts College on March 28, 1927.[65]

In the late 1920s the university's philosophy regarding student activities underwent a major change. For the first time in the university's history, open organizations for students became a vital part of campus life. Previously, all organizational membership was by invitation only. Even groups like the Lady Bugs and the Gold Bugs, who cheered at sporting events, accepted only a few new members each fall. Students earlier in the century had aspired to belong to closed organizations and viewed selection to one of these organizations as a place of honor. Around 1927, a movement began within the biology department, promoting the concept of "one world." Because of this new educational concept, students formed the first open pep organization, the Pepettes. Within one year, membership had nearly doubled and the face of campus organizations was forever changed. All students for the first time had the opportunity to join any number of organizations.[66]

In 1928 the Fine Arts Building was completed, boasting an auditorium that seated more than

1928 marked the greatest season yet for the Goldbugs. They tied for the state football championship and Roy Allen, Bill Moore, Perk Whitman, and Jack Alexander received positions on the All-State team.

1,400 people. The space was used for weekly chapel meetings, dramatic performances, and musicals. It also housed the Oklahoma City Symphony and Civic Theater.[67] Clarence A. Burg was selected as the first dean of the College of Fine Arts. Burg had previously performed with the New York Metropolitan Opera.[68]

Despite apparent success, the university reported to the West Oklahoma Annual Conference in November of 1928 that it had incurred $250,000 in debt since its establishment in 1919.[69] This debt would accumulate $186,000 in interest over the next three decades.

In 1929 the Methodist-Episcopal Church, North, and Methodist-Episcopal Church, South, officially united upon the Methodist-Episcopal Church, South's payment of the $50,000 security it agreed to in 1926. This would be the first time the two branches were officially unified since 1911.[70]

Learning in lean times: Top row, from
left: A Tri-Beta member stands near a
geological formation; a young couple
poses for a photo, 1930. Middle row,
from left: A member of Tri-beta holds
a sieve during their annual trip; 1937
student council members review
legislation; Bottom row, from left: Tri
Beta members spend time in recreation;
Tri-Beta members experience outdoors
and cooking; the 1938 *Scarab* yearbook
chronicled students' experiences.

THE
Lean Years

1929 brought the stock market crash to the United States and an oil boom to Oklahoma. While Oklahoma City University and the state of Oklahoma did not feel the effects of the crash immediately, the university found itself often lacking the financial support needed to continue serving the community and the church. Members of faculty and staff took several pay-cuts over the next year, with some members receiving no pay at all.

Kamp's Brothers Grocery Store helped the university by providing members of faculty and staff food on credit, to be paid whenever money became available. The Methodist Church and Oklahoma City also came to the university's aid many times during the economic depression. On several occasions, the university made a plea to the church for donations from its members in order to ease financial distress.

Oklahoma City University students looked for ways to earn money during the economic downturn, as well. Many members of the university's football team took firefighting jobs to make ends meet. More classes were held late in the day so students could work and continue attending school at the same time.

These changes did not, however, prevent the school from holding its first opera season, beginning new programs, and creating new ways of meeting the changing needs of its students. In 1939, Oklahoma City University's first comprehensive history was completed by Reverend H. E. Brill. By the end of the 1930s, the university was still struggling financially, but enrollment was increasing and Oklahoma City University had seen its way through some of the toughest times in its history.

Right: The downtown college replaced the evening school. Facing page: New Oklahoma City University graduates march through the rain.

The Lean Years

The success of the Oklahoma City oil field, which opened in 1929, sustained the Oklahoma economy for a short time after the crash of the stock market in October 1929. In spite of its rocky financial history, the university remained relatively unfazed for a period following the crash, as well. Yet, it was during the following decade that the golden age of Oklahoma City University drew to a close.

Oklahoma City University kicked off its third decade of service with a visit from John D. Rockefeller, who called the university "potentially one of the greatest educational opportunities in the country." Rockefeller stated, ". . . the Christian College is the most permanent and productive of all forms of investment."[1] Oklahoma City University remained virtually unaffected by the stock market crash for the remainder of 1929, and in the fall of 1930, the university welcomed the largest freshmen class in its history.[2]

While enrollment was at an all-time high, the campaign for the endowment was postponed until the following school term due to the financial situation around the state and across the nation.[3] Members of the administration, as well as university faculty, took a ten percent cut in salary in addition to the five percent they had been donating to the university over the preceding five years.[4] Some faculty members with other sources of income gave up regular salaries altogether for the sake of the

institution. President Antrim called an emergency faculty meeting shortly after the stock market crash. He informed the faculty that there was only a small amount of money at the university's disposal; it was unknown when more would be available. Antrim divided the money among the faculty and staff as fairly as possible, allocating more for faculty who were supporting their families and less for those who were being supported by a spouse or family member. Some faculty members did not receive payment for many years following the crash. Kamp's Brothers Grocery Store at Northwest 25th Street and Classen Boulevard sold produce and other perishable items to members of the Oklahoma City University faculty and staff on credit with the understanding that the money would be collected when they could pay.[5] These substantial sacrifices were more than goodwill gestures. They ultimately saved the institution from bankruptcy.[6] The economic uncertainty of the years to come could not have been estimated, nor could the sacrifices made by Oklahoma City University faculty and staff be measured.

In September of 1930, Chief George Goff of the Oklahoma City Fire Department suggested that university athletes work for the fire department. The "firefighting athletes," as they became known, lost few games the following season.[7] This program provided money for the athletes to help pay their education and provided able bodies to perform the work of the

Six Degrees of Beethoven
Dean Clarence A. Burg

Contributed By Cassidy Logan Elms

"Keep busy. Don't stop going when you retire. Don't expect favors and don't tell your age."[1] Whenever a student at Oklahoma City University needed advice, Dr. Clarence A. Burg nearly always told them to stay busy. Burg's determination to stay active influenced many people and had an impact on Oklahoma City University.

Born in Dallas City, Illinois, and raised in the small town of DeQueen, Arkansas, as a boy Burg dreamed of being outside with his friends playing baseball. His mother would let him, only after he finished practicing piano. [2]

Burg went on to study piano at many schools, from Maryland to Illinois, to England, he studied at top schools.[3] When he traveled to Oklahoma City for a concert in 1928, he was invited to be the dean of fine arts and professor of piano at a local college.[4] At 35, Burg decided to teach at Oklahoma City University.[5] Florence Birdwell, who worked part-time for the school as a vocal instructor under Burg, recollects how "he ran it with an iron fist." Dean Burg kept meticulous records on the operation of the school. Birdwell, also a student of his, remembered him as a stringent teacher who helped her learn great technique.

Burg ran the music school with precision and optimism. During the Great Depression, Burg helped the university survive by being a very influential recruiter.[6] One of his famous stories from the depression was included in the spring 1987 issue of *Focus*.

> OCU owed Burg $1,800 in back salary, so Burg was unable to pay the mortgage on his home. The mortgage holder was Dr. G. A. Nichols, an OCU trustee, business man and founder of the upscale Nichols Hills section of Oklahoma City. Nichols had made a pledge to OCU of $2500. He could not pay the pledge because so many people, like Burg, whose mortgages he held, were unable to pay them. Burg devised a plan, which was approved by the OCU administration. OCU credited Nichols with $1,800 on his mortgage, and OCU no longer owed Burg his back salary. No money changed hands; everyone benefited.[7]

Not only did Burg help his school survive the depression, he made sure his students were well equipped. Barely at the school for one year, Dean Burg made improvements on the Fine Arts Building for both the music and art students.

In 1944 he secured national accreditation for the School of Music, making Oklahoma City University a part of the National Association of Schools of Music.[8] Burg left behind many accomplishments. He made sure the music school was in top condition, started a music camp in the Ozarks, joined the music school with the Civic Music Association in Oklahoma City, started the National Guild of Piano Teachers auditions in Oklahoma, and conducted many, many performances. Joining with the Civic Music Association, Burg made it possible for Civic Music to present concerts in the Kirkpatrick Auditorium at no cost as long as university students, faculty, and staff, could attend free of charge.[9]

When Burg conducted, it was no ordinary concert. He organized an annual festival where piano

students came to play together. Burg fit as many grand pianos, or sometimes upright pianos, on whatever stage he was using, and students performed in duets or groups. In one concert 1,100 performers performed on 25 grand pianos.

Another musician inspired by Burg is university piano instructor, Dr. Linda Owen. Owen wrote her dissertation on Burg and in 1993 she helped the university community celebrate what would have been his 100th birthday.[10] She organized a concert with 13 grand pianos and hundreds of players. If Owen could use one word to describe Dean Burg it would be "enthusiastic." She recalled that he had enthusiasm over every aspect of his life, especially over Oklahoma City University and its future. [11]

Burg was a performer, conductor, and composer. He also had a Beethoven connection. From the fall of 1983 OCU *Focus* Magazine comes this explanation of who really taught Burg. "Beethoven taught Czerny, who taught Leschetizsky, who taught Paderewski, who taught Stojowski, who taught Burg." There were six degrees of separation between Beethoven and any of the thousands of students Burg taught. And Burg taught thousands, not only piano but how great one man can be. At the age of 71, Dean Burg could remember any former student flawlessly with specific details.[12]

To memorialize Burg after his retirement and his acceptance of the title dean emeritus, the university set up a scholarship fund in his name. Two months after celebrating his last birthday Burg passed away at the age of 93. Today Dean Burg lives on in the memories of people and forever through a small auditorium located in OCU's Kirkpatrick Fine Arts Building. Known as the Burg Auditorium, the Theatre Department at OCU stages approximately two productions per semester on the stage. The stage is also open for recitals and guest speakers. Dean Burg's liveliness and commitment to Oklahoma City University is fondly remembered. Dr. Clarence A. Burg touched students' lives just as his fingers graced the ivory keys of a piano, with impact and determination.

[1] "A Lifetime of Music: Dean Burg (1893-1986) Leaves Luminous Legacy," *OCU Focus*, spring 1987, 20-21.

[2] Ibid.

[3] Ibid. / "'Dean Burg Begins 37th Year with OCU School of Music," *OCU Focus*, 3 Aug. 1964, 10.

[4] "A Lifetime of Music: Dean Burg (1893-1986) Leaves Luminous Legacy," *OCU Focus*, spring 1987, 20-21.

[5] "A Lifetime of Music: Dean Burg (1893-1986) Leaves Luminous Legacy," *OCU Focus*, spring 1987, 20-21.

[6] Dr. Linda Joyce Owen, personal interview, 29 Jan. 2004.

[7] Linda Joyce Owen, "The Contributions of Clarence A. Burg to Piano Pedagogy," Diss., University of Oklahoma, 1997.

[8] "A Lifetime of Music: Dean Burg (1893-1986) Leaves Luminous Legacy," *OCU Focus*, spring 1987, 20-21.

[9] Dr. Linda Joyce Owen, personal interview, 29 Jan. 2004.

[10] "Celebration Honors Former Music School Dean," *OCU Focus*, fall 1993, 8.

[11] Dr. Linda Joyce Owen, personal interview, 29 Jan. 2004.

[12] "Dean Burg OCU's 'Beethoven Connection' Turns 90," *OCU Focus*, fall 1983, 10.

Up in a Blaze of Glory
OCU Athletes Moon-Light as Firemen
Contributed By Cassie J. Bennett

A three story red brick building rises up at California and Walker Avenue. Fire Station No. 1, the headquarters for all of Oklahoma City, displayed five apparatus doors each filled with a gleaming red engine. This is where the "the monsters of the gridiron," or as more often called, "The Big Bruisers" heroically fought fires for numerous years and several even sought fit to retire.[1] These men not only went to Oklahoma City University to gain an education but also dominated the field as part of the Goldbugs football team.

Fire Chief George B. Goff solicited the Goldbugs football team to work for the fire department because he simply "thought it a good idea."[2] They could go to school all day, work all night, and play football on the side. When it came to game nights the "Gridder-firemen," as they were called by many schools such as Central State Teachers College of Edmond, made special arrangements with the station.[3] Students from central, the night before the big game, would call in false alarms to keep them up all night so that they would be tired before the game.[4]

Throughout the years several groups of Oklahoma City University athletes have rushed through the fire station. In 1939, it was the Goldbugs varsity football team. In 1936, men such as Hoyt "Punny" Barton, Spec Wayland, Perry Griffin, and even coach, Hack Holt, from the varsity football team were employed by the fire department.[5] In 1934, men from the Goldbugs state champion baseball team served. They included Crusty Barton, Orville Kline, Cecil Jones, Haskell Holt, and Nim Newberry.[6]

The ones who started it all, though, were those varsity football players of 1930. Thirty-seven Oklahoma City University men worked at Fire Station No. 1, where all but two firemen were the amazing Goldbugs varsity football players.[7] Some nights seemed endless with call after call and extremely tiring work, while some were so incredibly slow that they slept the whole night through. According to the October 31, 1930, issue of *The Campus*, Clarence Asher, a reporter, described that the men saw periods of time in which fires broke out in quick succession and business boomed in comparison. The men worked from six o'clock in the evening until eight o'clock in the morning and somehow found it possible to juggle homework, sleep, practice, and saving lives. These football heroes were only awakened by alarms and for brief phone watches for incoming calls to the station.

As part of their job, the men found themselves doing theater duty on campus approximately once a week. Since the risk of a fire occurring was great, every night during a show one man did fire watch duty from seven until eleven. He sat backstage in the cold, dark Kirkpatrick Auditorium hoping and praying that no fire would occur. Then as the curtain dropped and the house lights came on, he wiped his brow in relief and knew his duties were finished and he could return home.

For their duties at the station they received a reliable monthly paycheck. As for their services at the theatre they received two additional rewards. They received a reliable paycheck once a month and Clarence Asher reported that, "every bus and street-car operator is the fireman's friend." None of the Goldbugs ever had to pay a fare to ride.

[1] Ron Moss, *A Century of Service: 1889-1989*.

[2] Ibid.

[3] Ibid.

[4] Ibid.

[5] "Bugs Face Unbeaten Sooners Here Today," Newspaper clipping in a scrapbook at the Oklahoma Fire Fighters Museum, 20 May 1936.

[6] "Oklahoma City University's State Championship Baseball Team," Ibid., c. 1934.

[7] Asher, Clarence, "Thirty-Seven Goldbugs Go to Blazes; Out All Night and Don't Go Home," *The Campus*, vol. XIII: October 31, 1930, 3.

The women of Beta Alpha Phi support the Goldbugs during homecoming, showing pride and displaying a banner during the 1935 homecoming parade.

fire department.[8] It was not uncommon for opponents to call in false alarms the night before a game, hoping to wear down the athletes.

Although times were lean and money was tight, Oklahoma City University continued to make progress as an institution. On April 4, 1930, the university opened its first annual opera season. Admission was fifty cents.[9] The following summer the university began working on a special project, the Taos Experiment, to provide Oklahoma students and teachers the opportunity to view art and scenery in New Mexico. However, because of the cost of travel and the economic downturn, the program attracted more students from New Mexico than Oklahoma. The program offered an average of ten classes per term and served approximately 282 students a year.[10]

Progress continued as the university ushered in the 1931-32 school year with the opening of a junior college located temporarily at Capitol Hill High School. The college offered students the opportunity to complete their first two years of college credit on a more flexible basis.[11]

Oklahoma City University saw great strides not only in academics, but in athletics as well. In 1931 the Goldbug track team claimed the title at the Big Four Conference.[12] The newly renamed Cardinals girls' basketball team boasted thirty-two wins in its first season under the direction of Sam F. Bobb.[13]

Although the university experienced many successes over the course of the school term, at the close of the 1931 fiscal year, the university needed $42,000 to balance the budget. This amount was in addition to already existing debt that had been incurred. The City of Oklahoma City offered $22,000 toward elimination of the budget deficit, the remaining $20,000 in expense would be divided evenly between the board of the Methodist-Episcopal Church, South, and the university. [14]

Students showed their school spirit at the university football games. Goldbug football players not only participated in classes and on the football team, but also often worked for the local fire department.

Oklahoma City University again appealed for funds during the 1932 annual conference, this time requesting $25,000 to reduce outstanding debt. The university also requested that a special appeal be made on its behalf to the Methodist-Episcopal Church congregations.[15]

In 1933 the Evening School was replaced by the new Downtown College. The Downtown College offered classes five evenings a week instead of the two the Evening School had.[16] While this was considered another advancement for the institution, Oklahoma City University still struggled financially. The university again made an appeal to the local church, setting a goal of a quarter per member to help alleviate some of the financial difficulty the university had experienced since the start of the Great Depression four years earlier.[17]

University finances showed little improvement in 1934, although enrollment was rising and programs were once again beginning to grow.[18]

Walter Scott Athearn was inaugurated as university president on June 22, 1934.[19] His presidency ended less than five months after his inauguration, when, while on university business in St. Louis, Missouri, Athearn suffered a heart attack and died on November 13.[20]

A.G. Williamson, president of the board of trustees, succeeded Athearn in the office of president. Williamson was the first alumnus to serve as the head of the university. Williamson graduated from Oklahoma Methodist University in 1916.[21] When elected university president, he was pastoring the Wesley Methodist Church, as well as serving the Oklahoma City District of the Methodist-Episcopal Church as district superintendent.[22]

While Williamson seemed to meet all the criteria for the university's highest administrative post, his transition into office was less than smooth. When students learned the board of trustees was selecting a new president, they presented the board with a petition containing more than 300 signatures requesting that Dean T. A. Williams be named the next president. The names on the petition had been secured in just two hours. Although the effort proved unsuccessful, Dean Williams later thanked the students, stating:

> I never sought the presidency of OCU. I have preferred to stay in my place and do the work that is mine to do without interference or embarrassment . . . I have always been an ardent believer in the large possibilities of OCU. It was the challenging character of these that lured me away from an agreeable and permanent position on the faculty of one of the oldest and most honored institutions of the Methodist Church . . . I am still convinced . . . that a great future is possible for our university.[23]

Whatever its potential for greatness, the fact remained that money was in short supply at the university. The university again made an appeal to area Methodist churches for twenty-five cents per member in an attempt to balance the budget.[24]

In 1935 Oklahoma City University amended its articles of incorporation and revamped its academic program.[25] The College of Liberal Arts' new academic program was divided into two specific areas. The first area, the general college, focused on freshmen and sophomore students and gave an overview of all areas of study. The second area, the senior college, represented specific areas of scholarship. The senior college was further divided into four general areas of study: language, literature and speech; natural science and math; social sciences; and philosophy, psychology, education, religious education, health and physical education.[26]

While the Oklahoma City campus reorganized its curriculum in 1935, the Taos Project ended after

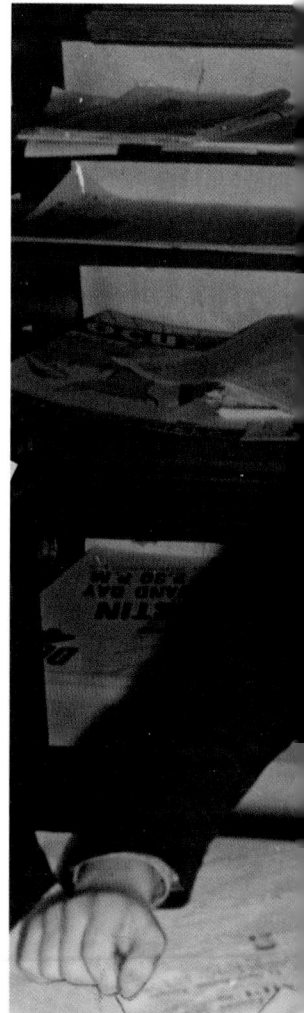

five years. The program had better served students of New Mexico than those of Oklahoma and had not met the goals of the institution. Furthermore, Oklahoma City University did not have a charter to educate in the State of New Mexico and withdrew from the Taos Project for fear of creating ill relations with the academic community in the area.[27]

In March, 1936, Oklahoma City University celebrated its silver jubilee with special services held in area Methodist-Episcopal churches. On March 17, the date on which the university had actually been brought to life, a two-hour program was presented in the university chapel to commemorate and recount the institution's history. [28]

Wishard Lemons, left, described in the 1939 *Scarab* as a "carefree redhead" led *The Campus* staff with Melvin Shepard as his business manager. The staff challenged the administration frequently on the issue of censorship.

In 1939 the university welcomed golden gloves boxer Marvin Lindell to the coaching staff. Lindell was known both nationally and internationally. He held 18 boxing titles at the time he was hired to coach the university boxing team.[29] That spring, Reverend H. E. Brill, who managed the university printing press completed Oklahoma City University's first comprehensive history.[30]

For nearly fifteen years Oklahoma City University had "passed from one crisis to another but continued to survive when many of the strong institutions of America went down in the thirties," wrote Brill.[31] As another decade of Christian education in the capital city drew to a close, the years ahead looked more hopeful. By the end of the 1930s, Oklahoma City University's financial situation was less than ideal, but enrollment had steadily increased. The university always seemed poised on the cusp of greatness, awaiting the dawn of a renaissance.

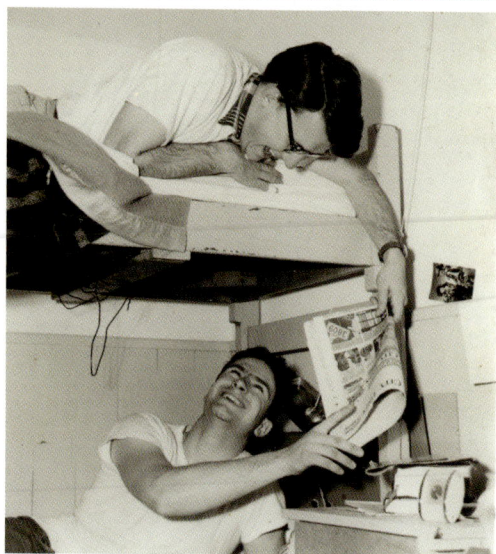

Learning discipline, making traditions: Top row, from left: students move between classes at the Downtown School; members of the 344th Military detachment exercise. Middle row, from left: Students perform during Leap week; 1946, young women learn the art of dressmaking; and plans for the Gold Star Memorial Building are made. Bottom row, from left: Jim Morris, composer of the Alma Mater; Oklahoma City University students enjoyed on-campus living for the first time; family members of gold star recpients attend a dedication service in the Goldbug Gymnasium.

WAR and Growth

World War II brought significant changes to the nation and to the Oklahoma City University campus in December, 1941. C.Q. Smith became president of Oklahoma City University at a crucial time in the university's history; the nation struggled under a season of instability and, the university required aggressive leadership and swift decision-making. Smith worked quickly during his first few months in office to plan for the university's future and solve problems that required his immediate attention. Buildings were erected almost overnight and campus housing became an option for students for the first time in the university's history.

Because of World War II, the university began offering courses in defense and, the 344th military detachment became a significant part of campus life. In spite of the war, enrollment continued to grow. The endowment grew and Oklahoma City University began to flourish once again.

Oklahoma City University emerged from The Depression with great debt, but by May, 1944 the university was free from debt once again. After only three years the bank note was burned during commencement. In 1946, the university mascot was changed to the chief after only a few weeks as the thunderbird.

Athletics made a comeback following the war as GIs flooded the university campus. Once again, the university moved swiftly to accommodate the influx of new students. Classes were held in church buildings and temporary locations until the appropriate space could be acquired. By 1949, a monument to the Oklahoma Methodists who had fallen in World War II, the Gold Star Memorial Building, was being constructed.

C. Q. Smith, who was president of the university for 16 years, focused on building community and tradition on campus as well as expanding the university's grounds and faculty.

The Smith Years

As Oklahoma City University emerged from the Great Depression, it stood shakily on the edge of both failure and success. In 1940, Jim Morris, a senior music student, wrote the university hymn, *Hail, Alma Mater*. This substantial development was one of many changes that occurred in the early part of the decade.

Another significant change occurred shortly after President Franklin Roosevelt declared a national state of emergency on May 28, 1941, as war continued to rage in Europe and in the Pacific.[1] With the world torn by war, and the future of nation still unsure, Oklahoma City University ushered in a new president.[2] The battery of problems that greeted Dr. C. Q. Smith on his first day in office in the summer of 1941 included a budget to balance, a note due to the First National Bank that day, and a $450,000 debt.[3] Professor Peter W. Swartz, at the time doubling as the university's business manager, told Smith faculty and staff salaries were again overdue and there was no money to pay them.[4]

Smith met with the executive committee of the board of trustees that afternoon and notified them of the unpaid salaries. For several years loyal faculty and staff had taken pay cuts and accepted compensation in the form of produce and any other goods the university could offer. For the second

A Family in Service

The Harrison Brothers Fight Together

Contributed By A. Dunaway

Many outstanding university students and alumni served in World War II from coast to coast and overseas. Three of these young men were the Harrison brothers.

In 1927 Oklahoma City University welcomed its first Harrison brother, William. He began a family tradition when he rushed for Delta Psi Omega. He was also active in the Scorpion Pep Club and Pep Council while at the university. William graduated with an Bachelor of Arts degree in 1931.

Before his fellow classmates could forget William, they were introduced to his younger brother, Arthur, who enrolled in 1932. Arthur also rushed Delta Psi Omega, but he took it a step farther when he became president of the fraternity. Arthur also ran and won the office of freshman class president, junior class president, and president of the Inter-Fraternity Council, and was a member of the debate team. When he graduated in 1935, Arthur was named Most Respected Boy at Oklahoma City University.

1937 marked the graduation of the last Harrison brother when Robert Harrison became an alumnus. Robert carried on the family tradition by being active in Delta Psi Omega. He was a leader. Like his brother Arthur, Robert became the 1934 freshman class president, the same year Arthur was junior class president. He was also active in Blue Key, Beta Upsilon Sigma, Dance Board, and deputy archon.

Seven years after graduation, the Harrison name was once again gracing the pages of the The Campus in 1944. Just as all brothers had shared the same fraternity, they were sharing the honor of serving their country. The headline of the March 31, 1944, edition of The Campus read, "Three Former O.C.U. Brothers in Service." William was a major, stationed in England, Arthur served as an ensign, stationed in Los Angeles, California, and Robert was a field artillery lieutenant serving in Breckenridge, Virginia.

The Harrison brothers' college days had been profoundly affected by the experience of World War I. Memories of losing loved ones and living in fear fostered anti-war sentiments nationwide. In 1935, more than 175,000 American college students went on strike in protest of war. Observers wondered whether or not the young people merely "lacked guts." However, one campus reporter observed that the New York Post "pats us on the back for our demonstration against war and generally takes it for granted that we will defend our country despite all our resolutions to the contrary."[1]

However, after December of 1941, The Campus was printing a different perspective on war. The following year's evidence that university students' views of war had changed could be found in every issue of The Campus. Each paper was peppered with enlistment propaganda and encouragements to buy war stamps.

William, Arthur, and Robert were quick to take up arms in defense of their country. The university may not have directly influenced them to join the services, but it did teach them about leadership and commitment. With these valuable tools gained from Oklahoma City University, the Harrison brothers took their legacy from their campus to their country.

[1] "War and Students," The Campus, 17 Oct. 1935.

month in row, faculty salaries were to be delivered late. Once the board became aware of the situation's urgency, several board members pledged their own money to ensure the faculty and staff were paid on time. Trustees V. V. Harris and Newton Avery borrowed money on their own signatures to guarantee the checks due to the university staff.[5]

Smith's presidency was marked by aggressive action. In his first matriculation address, Smith stated "laziness [was] responsible for more failures than all other causes."[6] Within one week of taking office, Smith announced a plan to erect the first permanent dormitories on campus.[7] Before the start of the fall term, Smith had the Tabernacle Dining Room converted into a men's dormitory which held 28 students and renamed it Epworth Hall. The Goldbug Gym was also transformed into a men's dormitory for an additional forty-two students, and the Lambda Chi house, located at the corner of Northwest 23rd Street and Indiana Avenue, was remodeled to create a home for twenty-four women.[8] By October of 1941, Smith had added student health services on campus and approved a $50,000 building campaign for new dormitories, lab facilities, a rebuilt stadium, tennis courts, and a golf course.[9]

A primary academic goal for Smith was the long-sought North Central Accreditation. To receive this prestigious and critical endorsement, the university needed to substantially increase its endowment and the number of volumes contained in its library.[10]

In October, 1941 the Methodist Church of Oklahoma voted to award the university an assured $25,000 "living endowment."[11] These monies would be paid yearly to the institution. Oklahoma City University was one step closer to receiving the coveted North Central Accreditation. In addition to the growing endowment, partially funded by the Methodist Conference, local Methodist churches collected a yearly special offering between 1941 and 1949 to help offset the operating costs of the university.[12]

Not only was money being raised for the construction of new buildings on campus and the endowment, but enrollment increased steadily, and for the first time since the early 1930s, Oklahoma City University's athletic program was being enlarged. In efforts to save money during the Great Depression, many sports had been eliminated. As the financial situation of the university stabilized, Oklahoma City University sponsored not only mainstream athletics such as football and basketball, but less profitable sports like golf, tennis, track, and boxing.[13]

In a short time, Oklahoma City University took monumental strides. Then on December 7, 1941, the United States was attacked by the Japanese at Pearl Harbor. At 10:00 that morning, the entire student body assembled in the University Chapel, and Smith reviewed the events of the morning with both students and faculty. A vote was held, asserting that the students of Oklahoma City University were committed to keeping the institution alive, no matter what the cost.[14] For the second time in the university's history, its students would march

Construction on the Gold Star Memorial Building took several years. When it was completed the building stood as a symbol honoring the lives of young Methodists who were killed defending the country during World War II.

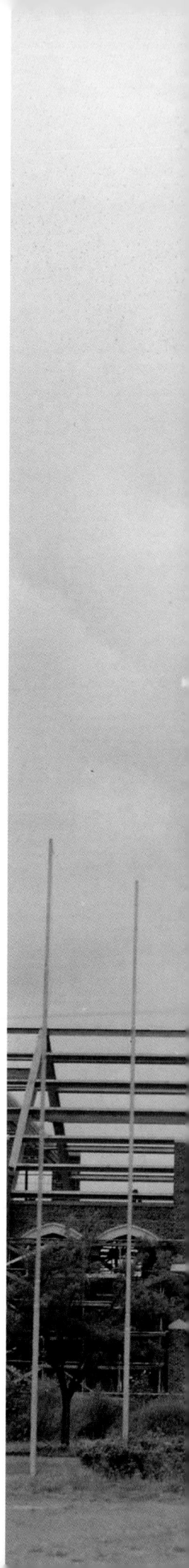

Teacher Gives Generously
Irminda Banning Bequeaths Estate to University

Contributed By Lyall C. Storandt

The early spring days of 1943 were a precarious time for a university in danger of being seized by its mortgager. Oklahoma City University was more than $300,000 in debt and in poor financial condition. All of that changed when university President C. Q. Smith received an unexpected phone call from Irminda Banning. Miss Banning, a retired school teacher and native of Ohio, informed the president of her wish to donate to the university a memoriam for her sister, Sophia. Smith and Banning agreed to meet and discuss the matter at 10:00 a.m. the next day.[1]

Banning arrived at the meeting with her tax receipts for five businesses, five homes, and five apartment buildings. Her initial wish, in her own words, was "…to give to the university the Cain Coffee Building at Northeast 12th Street and Santa Fe Avenue to erect a building in memory of my sister, Sophia."[2] Smith explained the university's financial situation and advised her to proceed with caution. In his book, *Building for Tomorrow* Smith recalled sending the following memo to Banning:

1. Gift should be protected against loss or dissipation.
2. Donor should be protected from need or want.
3. Should be invested to the best interest of humanity.
4. Should carry worthy or appropriate memorial.

Miss Banning, these four points deserve your considerations in the matter discussed yesterday.

Signed,
C. Q. Smith.[3]

That same afternoon Banning called to schedule another meeting for the next morning. On April 2, 1943, Smith presented her with an endowed scholarship plan.

There were several conditions for the gift: The university was to pay Banning a stipulated monthly amount for life. It was to provide all the scholarships that the interest from the gift would support at $300 per year per student. No part of the gift could ever be loaned to the university or mortgaged. And, a bronze plaque was to be placed in the Great Hall as a memorial to the Banning sisters. The contract for the gift was drawn up with a provision calling for special trustees of the fund due to the financial instability of the university. President Smith suggested, in lieu of the special trustees, a stipulation stating that if the university ceases to exist the Banning Foundation would become the property of the General Board of Education of the Methodist Church. This provision would allow for the foundation to exist as long as there was, according to Smith, "one Methodist in the world."[4] This pleased Banning, and she signed the contract. She advised her attorney to draft her will leaving anything left of her estate to the foundation. However, she never signed the revised will.

On April 13, 1943, the university trustees accepted the foundation and the final contract was presented to Banning for signing before a notary. The next day, Banning suffered a heart attack while shopping in downtown Oklahoma City. It was at this juncture that things began to get complicated. Banning's great nephew, Freddie Ansil, alerted President Smith of her condition early on the morning of April 15. Smith rushed to the hospital and joined Ansil in overseeing the care being given to Banning by heart specialist Dr. Wann Langston, who later testified that Banning was capable of transacting her business. Smith made daily visits to the hospital, but only once did he mention

the foundation. On the eve of her death, Banning said to Smith, "I want you to take that foundation and administer it."[5] Irminda Banning died at 3:00 a.m. on Sunday, April 18, 1943. After her death, Banning's relatives in Ohio, who apparently were not informed of her wishes, sued the university to break the foundation contract. According to Smith, Banning's relatives employed the president of the Oklahoma City Bar Association, Tom Garrett, and an attorney from Philadelphia to represent them in the ensuing court case. Smith's book details how the university hired V. P. Crowe and C. Harold Thweatt of the firm Embry, Johnson, Tolbert and Crowe to defend them in district court. Judge Clarence Mills rendered a decision in favor of the university in the case. That decision was appealed to the Oklahoma State Supreme Court, where it remained in litigation for three more years before a final verdict in favor of the university was handed down in 1947. Following the court decision, the less fruitful properties were sold and the proceeds invested, while the Cain Coffee Building and two main street stores were retained.[6]

In his annual report to the East Oklahoma Conference of the Methodist Church called the previous year phenomenal. He cited enrollment, the payment of the long-standing in 1943, Smith a 100 percent increase in $300,000 indebtedness, the half-million dollar endowment gift from Banning, and the university's operation without a deficit as reasons for the great year. 1947 became the first year that the foundation, which was now valued at $450,000, awarded 20 scholarships worth a total of $1,200 each payable as $300 a year over a four year period. At the time, any student graduating in the upper 15 percent of their class and with an intelligence quotient of 110 or more was qualified to compete for the awards. The effects of this generous donation are still visible on the campus today as one of the women's dormitories is named in honor of the Banning sisters and their plaque still hangs in the Great Hall.

[1] Smith, 147.

[2] Ibid.

[3] Smith, 148

[4] Smith, 150.

[5] Smith, 152.

[6] Ibid.

off to war to defend the rights and way of life of the American people.[15]

The university's Capella Choir was heard in a national broadcast on a half-hour program over NBC Radio in Chicago, Illinois, during a trip taken between December 28, 1941 and January 10, 1942.[16]

In January, following the outbreak of World War II, C. Q. Smith was officially inaugurated as president of Oklahoma City University. Friday, January 16, 1942, began with the raising of the flag and a ceremony held in the university auditorium. Following the ceremony was a luncheon and a student art exhibit and tea. That evening a drama was presented by the University Players.[17] Smith would be the eighth man inaugurated as university president. His inaugural address was broadcast by nine Oklahoma radio stations.[18]

Smith, a Texan by birth, began his career in education as the principal of a country school, later serving as the superintendent of schools in Memphis, Texas. After several years of teaching, Smith entered into the ministry of the Methodist Church. He later became commissioner and general superintendent of hospital work for the Central Texas Conference. Smith built and readied Harris Memorial Hospital in Fort Worth, Texas, for use—a one million dollar accomplishment. He also served as the president of McMurry College in Abilene, Texas, and as a vice president of Southern Methodist University.[19]

Smith was well aware of the effects that the newly embarked upon war could have on the university in the long term:

> We have been in open war for less than two months, yet nine percent of college faculties in America have already been called from the classroom into defense services … and nine percent of them failed to return to school this semester. . . Financial assets are being frozen and priorities required for materials of all kinds. Government support of education is being confined to those courses most needed for defense. The whole world seems to be surging with uncontrolled passions, tumultuous with ungoverned greed, confused with unrelated ideals, frightened by threatened impending doom of the things cultured civilization holds dear.[20]

The War Program

In May 1942 more than 700 students were enrolled in Oklahoma City University's war program. The university was the first institution in the nation to establish courses for teachers that qualified them in the instruction of fundamentals of aeronautics. The university's detachment occupied the space that had been the 4H building and the Future Farmers of America (FFA) building on the Oklahoma State Fair Grounds. These buildings quickly metamorphosed into barracks for the participants in the flight training program.[21] Beginning in spring, 1943, defense courses were offered free of charge to any man or woman interested in military service.[22] Many of OCU's finest instructors gave their spare time to lend aid to the national defense program. Classes were offered through Civil Aeronautics Training in the areas of science and managing defense training groups. All instruction was paid for by the United States government.[23]

Young men came from across the country not only to enroll in regular college course work, but to take classes that would help them earn ranks in the United States Air Corps. The cadets' days began at 5:50 a.m. with breakfast served at 6:45 a.m. Classroom instruction began promptly at 8:00 a.m. with classes continuing until nearly 5:00 p.m. After dinner the cadets were allocated less than two hours of free time before a 10 p.m. bedtime. The fairgrounds underwent substantial changes during the period, creating facilities such as a full service kitchen, barber shop, canteen, and classrooms to accommodate the newly arrived cadets. [24] The university training grounds housed 500 cadets at a time and trained 1,100 cadets over the course of its two-year existence.[25]

In addition to the training detachment, the university purchased an airfield near the end of May, 1943 to be used only by students enrolled in the war program. The field was located six miles east of the capitol just off Northwest 23rd Street.[26]

On the Home Front

In spite of the war, enrollment during the 1942 school year was up,[27] although for the first time there were three times as many women as men on campus, with 72 percent of the men on campus either freshmen or sophomores and below the draft age. Because of the low number of men returning to campus in the fall of 1942, the football program was dropped from the sports schedule due to lack of participation.[28]

By 1943 half of the $450,000 debt that had existed when Smith assumed the office of president had been paid.[29]

A total of 477 Oklahoma City University alumni and students were enlisted in the United States Armed Forces.[30] A complete service roll hung in the university's Great Hall, listing 500 former students, nine of whom had received gold stars.[31]

Oklahoma City University received an award for its service to the United States Armed Forces in July, 1944. For several years the university had served both the armed

Eva Martin, right, manages crowds in the Goldbug cafeteria. The Goldbug building served many different functions throughout the institution's history and throughout the 1940s provided a space in which students could dine.

A Call to Arms
The 344th Training Detachment
Contributed By Gideon Keith-Stanley

In 1943, the world was at war. Nazi Germany had dominated most of Europe and Imperial Japan controlled much of the Pacific and Asia. Across the United States, citizens took a solemn pride in "doing their part" for the war effort. American wives lay down their aprons and picked up hard hats. Men and boys lay down their plows and picked up rifles. Among the Americans who so readily responded to their nation's call was Oklahoma City University President C. Q. Smith.

Before the war, Oklahoma City University had been one of the premier aeronautical institutes in the world.[1] Students flocked to the institution to become aeronautical technical instructors. When the military asked American institutions for help, Smith provided the leadership the university needed to answer the call to arms.

On April 7, 1943, Oklahoma City University received 500 air cadets for the Army and Navy Air Corps. Additional housing was needed, so several buildings at the fairgrounds were leased, along with Bethany Municipal Airport No. 2, later called Wiley Post Municipal Airport. New heating systems, as well as sanitary and culinary facilities were added to many of the buildings.

Many brave men were recruited from the rapidly growing capital city. Young men who qualified to enter pre-flight school would compete to get into the best schools, including Oklahoma City University. Upon arrival, these men would find themselves at the mercy of the institution's drill instructors, working them hard to make them fit for the fight ahead.

The 344th Training Detachment of the United States Army Air Corps made its home at Oklahoma City University. Army-approved instructors were employed and military doctrine was brought into the classroom. Many defense courses were offered, giving students and cadets the skills they would need to save lives in combat.

The university's students rallied behind the war cause by raising money with a war bond rally. Students went door to door to raise $8,386.75 in war bonds, and students postered the campus to raise awareness of the need for every single person to help. The money raised for war bonds would outfit aircraft, arm soldiers, and repair naval vessels.

Oklahoma City University trainees would go on to serve in combat air crews for "Flying Fortresses," bombing occupied France, Germany, Italy, and Japan. Of the 500 combat air crewmen who were trained, nine met their ends at the hands of the Axis powers. These brave men were awarded Gold Stars for their bravery and ultimate sacrifices for freedom. The Gold Star Memorial Building stands as a monument to the men and women of the Methodist Church who gave their lives for their country during World War II.

[1] *Brief description of Oklahoma City University prior to arrival of Training Detachment,* Smith, Clustor Quentin, personal correspondence, Special Collections Archives, Dulaney-Browne Library, Oklahoma City University, OK.

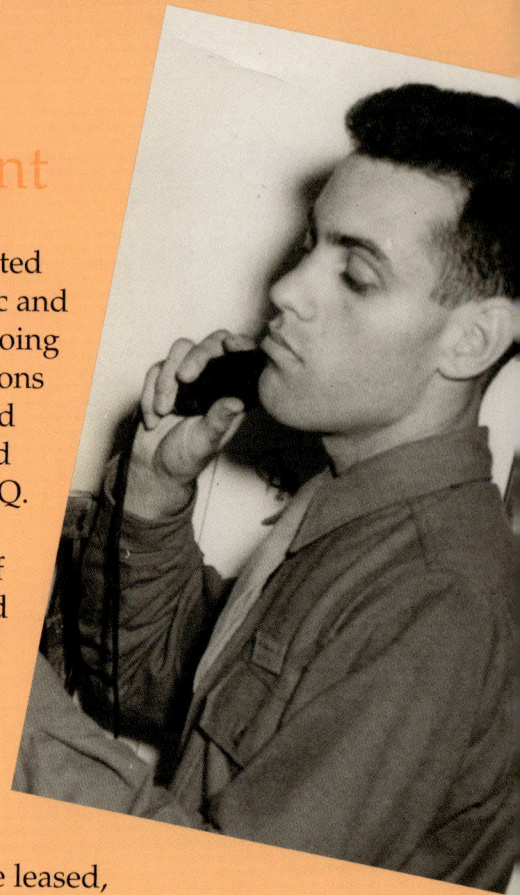

forces, and the nation by training 1,100 cadets in the 344th training detachment.[32]

In March, 1944 the university's School of Music received its national accreditation when it was accepted into the National Association of Schools of Music after a visit by the accrediting committee earlier in the year.[37]

Amid that year's celebration of commencement, and the symbolic passing from one part of life to the next, Oklahoma City University also underwent a rite of passage. As a part of the graduation exercises on May 23, 1944, President Smith, along with members of the Board of Trustees, burned the only remaining notes against the university. The burning of the notes served as a symbolic representation of Smith's ability to free the institution from debt.[38]

On June 23, 1944, a fund-raising campaign began to add 10,000 volumes to the university library. If the campaign goal was reached, Oklahoma City University would be another step closer to receiving the North Central Accreditation Smith had targeted as a priority three years earlier. The campaign sought $16,000 to purchase the books.[39]

Sororities on campus, as well as organizations for independent students, selected one girl to participate in a pin-up contest in December, 1944. The winners would be photographed by Brazilian actor and director Tito Guizar.[40] Guizar would select three girls from the pool of young women to be photographed. The winners would be placed in a showcase in the university's Great Hall. Selected for the contest were: Shirley Pyeatt from Alpha Omega Sorority; Dorothy Lee Carter of Beta Alpha Phi; Jone Wells, an independent; Joyce Rowley of Kappa Tau Delta; Beverly Crockett of Phi Delta; and Eleanor Kouri of Phi Phi Phi.[41]

The Administration Building was struck by lightning in the spring of 1945, requiring $1,000 in repairs. This marked the fourth time in eighteen years that the tower had been damaged by lightning, each time hitting a different spire of the tower.[42]

The End of the War

In 1945, as World War II finally drew to a close, Oklahoma City University was growing rapidly. In September, 1945, 900 GIs flooded the campus. The university had neither the space nor the resources to handle this sudden influx in enrollment and the institution had to begin exploring options for expansion. Space was rented from nearby Wesley Methodist Church to accommodate 600 students. For the first time since the war began, there was a greater number of men on campus than women; with enrollment topping-out at 60 percent male and only 40 percent female.[43] By the end of the spring term, there were 1,600 veterans enrolled at Oklahoma City University.[44]

A memorial was held on Wednesday, May 9, 1945, to commemorate 16 university students who lost their lives during the war.[45]

In December, 1945 former Oklahoma City University student Ann Steely signed a contract with MGM Studios. Hailed by gossip columnist Hedda Hooper as "the Oklahoma Beauty," Steely, whose stage name was Cathy O'Donnell, played her first Hollywood role as Wilma in *The Best Years of our Lives*, based on Mackinely Kantor's novel, *Glory for Me*. While at a Hollywood party, only two weeks after her arrival in California, Steely met MGM executives. Impressed with her talent and beauty, they requested that she participate in a screen test. As a result, Steely was cast in her first role. While at Oklahoma City University, Steely had starred in several campus productions and studied under Professor Wayne Campbell.[46]

Oklahoma City University's involvement with the United States Armed Forces did not end with the war. By mid-winter, 1946, the university's enrollment had reached an all-time

high of 2,040.[47] Of those, 1,325 students during the 1946-47 school year were war veterans.[48] In September, 1946 a proposal was submitted to the United States Government to erect an armory on university property. The land at Northwest 27th Street and Kentucky would be leased to the government for one dollar a year for no more than fifty years. The facility would be used for storage of equipment and training purposes.[49] Shortly after the agreement was sealed with the United States Navy, President Smith arranged for the transfer of twenty-seven buildings from Will Rogers Field to campus: twenty-five barracks, a mess hall, and a larger, two-story barrack. Upon the buildings' arrival to the campus, they were converted into living quarters for male students who were a part of the naval reserve program. Many Oklahoma City University veterans were housed in similar buildings at the air field. Small apartments rented for $33 to $37 per month and were available with one, two, or three bedrooms.[50]

In addition to purchasing new buildings for the campus, in September, 1946, the university also purchased its first computer. The large IBM was located in the registrar's office and was used to more efficiently track student records. With the university's rapid growth since the end of the war, the job of registrar had become increasingly more difficult. The system came complete with punch card functions and card sorters.[51]

For a brief period in the summer of 1946, the Oklahoma City University Goldbugs were known as the Thunderbirds. The change of mascot was approved by the alumni association and President Smith and was intended to honor the men who had served as a part of the 45th Infantry Division during World War II. It was determined, however, after only a few weeks that the mascot of the Thunderbird could not belong to OCU alone. The alumni association again sought an appropriate emblem to represent the university as it entered the second half of the twentieth century. After much discussion the association and President Smith agreed the Chief should serve as the new mascot.[52]

Among those athletes who would proudly wear the Chief as their mascot the following year were two well established tennis stars who had emerged on the Oklahoma City University campus the previous spring. George Counts and Earl Stewart were an unstoppable doubles team. Both men were former GIs and, prior to their service in the war had garnered an exceptional number of awards. Counts was the Oklahoma State Amateurs tennis champion for three years, and Stewart had been the all-city champion in Cleveland, Ohio, Pittsburgh, Pennsylvania and Cincinnati, Ohio. Counts and Stewart were ranked number one and two, respectively, during the 1946 tennis season. Stewart and Counts traveled the country, serving as goodwill ambassadors for Oklahoma City University as the university renewed tennis and other sports programs.[53]

While the tennis program enjoyed its revival, the football program was gearing up for its first fall season since the war began. In fall, 1946, football was again a vital part of the campus. Under the direction of Coach George Fredrickson, the Chiefs achieved the status of the highest scoring team in the nation.[54]

Four generations of university presidents, Presidents Smith, Williamson, Athearn, and Green, gather at graduation to burn Oklahoma City University's debt note, recognizing that the university was debt-free only a few years after C. Q. Smith took office.

The following fall, President Smith undertook possibly the most monumental project of his career at the university. To memorialize those Oklahoma Methodists who had fallen in the Second World War, Smith began a $500,000 fund-raising campaign to erect the Gold Star Memorial Building at the heart of the Blackwelder campus. The project was officially announced in October, 1947 and promised a 270-foot tower of ten stories. The new building was to replace the existing Epworth Hall, which had served as a dormitory since Smith's arrival.[55] Groundwork began on the Gold Star Memorial Building on, October 10, 1949.[56]

At the beginning of the 1949-1950 school year, the big news on campus was the addition of a new business administration building, laundry, and heating plant, located near the center of campus. Estimated to be worth $250,000, the School of Business was expected to hold both business and industrial arts classes.[57] The university's downtown school also experienced great changes in late 1949 with its move to a larger building known as the Civic Center Campus. The downtown campus boasted an enrollment high of 1,100, and the new location allowed for growth. In the early years of the downtown school, it was solely a teachers' college.[58]

World politics was dominated by the emerging Cold War, as the United States and its allies squared off against the U.S.S.R. and its allies. Against this backdrop, the September 23, 1949, issue of *The Campus* student newspaper, told the story of Olga Molenke, an Estonian student who "ran from Communism," moving from place to place until finally landing in New York on July 3, 1949 and eventually studying at Oklahoma City University.[59] In March, 1950, the Student Senate refused to have a communist speak on campus, stating that, in doing so, they were supporting their own form of government while "maintaining a liberal attitude."[60]

Due to the value of oil and gas to Oklahoma's economy, a new class in oil and gas conservation became a popular class choice among geology students at the downtown campus. The course was designed jointly by the university and oil industry leaders to educate students on well spacing, oil and gas rights, and oil recovery methods.[61]

Dorm life helped to build community on the Oklahoma City University campus throughout the 1940s. The first men's dorm was erected on campus during this period and allowed convenient access to the university campus.

The campus matures and athletics grow: Top row, from left: Jerry Potter tosses a football during a routine practice; the ladies of Pennington Hall pause on the front stoop after engaging in athletics. Middle row, from left: St. Luke's Methodist Church maintained a relationship with the university throughout its history; books following the library fire of 1954; Jennie Pollard, the first African-American student's matriculation card filled out prior to graduation. Bottom row, from left: *The Pioneer Preacher*, erected during Smith's presidency made its home outside the Administration Building; two basketball players help an injured teammate off the court.

OUR

Community

The university continued to grow through the 1950s. Athletics played a more important role on campus and community became a greater focus. Oklahoma City University's relationship with the Methodist church remained strong as faith and scholarship were a central part of each student's educational experience.

As the university became a stronger community and a more cohesive environment, the board of trustees made a significant decision in Oklahoma City University's history. The board made the decision to integrate the campus, making the university a truly open learning environment.

More dorms were added to the campus as well as a student-faculty center, a physical plant, and bookstore.

The university celebrated it golden anniversary in 1954. Students and faculty alike paused momentarily to reflect on the institution's past.

The Cold War also played a vital role in the lives of students. Fear of invasion and communism were in the forefronts of collegiate minds.

During the 1950s Oklahoma City University made strides both socially and technologically. President Smith focused on building the campus physically and promoting comradary among students.

As the world rapidly changed, students explored the possibilities that their tomorrows held and hoped for a better future.

Librarians and students worked diligently to salvage the remains of the burned books after the fire which destroyed the north side of the building and damaged 14,000 volumes. Faculty, administration, and the board of trustees worked feverishly over the course of the next few months to replace the necessary books.

The November, 1950 Alumni-Varsity Classic basketball game was a bit bigger than usual, as the halftime entertainment included the crowning of an Alumni Queen. The queen was chosen based on how many tickets were sold by her active and alumni sorority. Three sororities named candidates, Alpha Omega, Beta Alpha Phi, and Phi Delta.[1] Margene Arnett, Phi Delta sorority alumna, was crowned Queen of the Alumni.[2] December of 1950 brought about the open house of the newly-built Pennington Hall, expected to accommodate 140 female students.

C.Q. Smith addressed alumni regarding the Christmas season:

> "'God bless us everyone,'" the immortal words of Tiny Tim, is being echoed around the world wherever there is a Christian this Christmas, 1950. Today, in a war torn world, where the star in the East is from an artillery piece, Christmas can easily have only a hollow meaning. It is up to you and me, and institutions like OCU dedicated to promulgating the ideals of the Child whose birth we celebrate December 25, to keep alive the real meaning and spirit of Christmas."[3]

In 1951, it cost $150 per semester for a student to attend Oklahoma City University,[4] and "Send us your son in '51" was the theme of the January 1951 *Oklahoma City University Bulletin*, seeking more alumni involvement in the alumni association and in promoting the university. 1951 was also the year the North Central Association of Colleges and Secondary Schools finally accepted the university for accreditation, and a great banquet was held to celebrate this great distinction.[5]

On June 2, 1951, a fire destroyed 14,000 books in the library, causing $15,000 in damage. In an early morning fire, the entire collection of philosophy, psychology, journalism, sociology, and religion books was lost.[6]

The alumni association immediately organized the "Book or Better Club" to raise money to replace lost books; those who donated money or books to the school through the drive were named members of the "Book or Better Club."[7] For months, the *Oklahoma City University Bulletin* published letters from alumni offering their money, books, and best wishes to the university and the library.

The eventful semester and Smith's efforts to strengthen the university was publicized as Mayor Allen Street proclaimed the week of September 30 to October 7, 1951, "Oklahoma City University Week," which included a banquet held to honor Smith for his ten years of service to the university.[8] The *Oklahoma City University Bulletin* reported that the Mutual Broadcasting System, the Trans-Canada Network, and the Armed Forces Network broadcasted the Oklahoma City Symphony from the university's fine arts auditorium weekly. The University Choir was also

Above left: Students celebrate an athletics victory during a traditional staged walkout. Walkouts were a part of the university tradition for many years and were held to commemorate victories or student achievements. Above right: A female student asks for two tickets during Leap Week, a time when male and female students switched gender roles.

featured from time to time.[9] On Sunday night, December 23 at 10:00 p.m., in a televised event, the star on the Gold Star Memorial Building was lit for the first time.[10]

In January 1952, the Chiefs men's basketball team won the all-college championship for the second time in three years.[11] Soon after, the university announced plans to purchase an old YMCA building for $300,000 to establish a law school at the downtown campus. The university considered establishing a law school by consolidating the privately owned Oklahoma City College of Law.

An executive committee of the university's board of trustees reviewed the university's status that year and identified the immediate needs of the university. Funds were needed for completion of the interior of the Gold Star Memorial Building whose exterior was funded by the Oklahoma Conference of the United Methodist Church, facilities for a veterans' education program, establishment of a school of law, a permanent home for the downtown school, various improvements on campus, and an addition to the fine arts building.[12]

Dr. Smith planned a $1,240,000 drive to expand and improve Oklahoma City University.[13] Luther T. Dulaney, president of Dulaney's Manufacturing Co., agreed to be the campaign general chairman, and C. R. Anthony became chairman of the Advisory Committee. The drive was planned for April and May of 1952. Dulaney and others focused on big gift donors.[14] The university acquired Oklahoma City College of Law at the end of the spring semester, and beginning in fall, 1952, the university had a law school downtown with a fall enrollment of 234 students, making it the largest law school in the state."[15]

During the 1951-1952 school year, Dr. John Peters, assistant professor in the Department of Religion, began World Assistance, Inc.[16] During a leave of absence from the university, Peters established the program to help people in underprivileged areas help themselves by providing training, tools,

medicines, seed, and livestock. The program helped people in impoverished areas move toward self-sufficiency.[17]

Oklahoma City University began the 1952-1953 school year with pride, knowing the university had been accredited and its prestige was growing.[18] A university alumnus, Hugh Taylor was a member of the Washington Redskins professional football team, and Archie Wiles, a music student and Fulbright Fellowship winner, appeared in a final recital at the university before moving on to study at the Verdi Conservatory of Music in Milan, Italy.[19]

In fall, 1952, college students throughout the nation were asked to assist the "Civilian Saucer Investigation" by reporting any sightings of "flying saucers." The official magazine of the Methodist Student Movement encouraged its readers to get involved. Students and scientists alike anticipated the outcome of a visit from creatures from another planet.[20] Meanwhile, the campus' Greek organizations were planning an all Greek "ribbon" dance to unite the organizations and present new pledges to the groups.[21]

Important politically to students was the issue of socialism—a topic of films, discussions, and student movements—as fear of socialism was common in the United States.[22] Tuberculosis also was responsible for American anxiety, and free chest x-rays were available for Oklahoma City University students.[23]

After five years of planning and work, on September 28, 1953, the library on the first and second floors of the Gold Star Memorial Building was formally opened.[24] With this new building came a new school year and a celebration of 50 years of higher education by the Methodist church in Oklahoma. The yearbook theme was "Fifty Years of Growth," and students focused on Oklahoma City University's history and ideals. Among the university ideals students noted were:

> An academic understanding is a prerequisite of any real college
> education. Without it, one can be superbly educated and yet,
> not learned….This is a Christian nation and a personal faith is
> very important. In view of this, it would be remarkable indeed
> if the student at OCU should not acquire an abiding religious
> realization in the course of his learning. This individual
> renaissance serves to strengthen his recognition of the supreme
> power higher than that of man.[25]

In November of 1953, the Korean Ambassador to the United States, Dr. You Chan Yang, addressed the OCU chapel audience about communism and Korea. He said he believed the Soviet Union was targeting Korea. "The communists are using a powerful propaganda machine to gain their ends," he continued. "They have pointed out that North Korea alone has defeated the United States and even the United Nations."

The year was distinguished by the formation of the Oklahoma City University Women's Council and the School of Industrial Arts. The women's council was formed for "the promotion of a keener awareness and a deeper appreciation of Oklahoma City University as a distinguished educational institution vitally important to the culture and general welfare of the community and state."[26] The School of Industrial Arts made Oklahoma City University the first university in the United States to offer a four year certificate in Industrial Arts, and the library was redesigned to house students seeking certification in industrial arts.[27]

On June 16, 1954, fire engulfed the center of campus, destroying the student union, gymnasium, book store, physical plant, and industrial arts building. Over a three-day period after the fire, approximately 30,000 people visited the scene.[28] Churches, businesses, and individuals began raising funds for reconstruction. By October, 1954, the School of Industrial Arts was near

In June of 1954 the
Oklahoma City
University campus was
once again plagued
by fire. This time the
destruction was greater,
damaging and
destroying several
campus buildings,
including the
gymnasium seen at right.

A Super Man
Herbert Bagwell and His Musical Gypsies
Contributed By Traci Ann Bair

Violinist Herbert Bagwell and comic book star Superman have one thing in common—a double identity. While Clark Kent was an ordinary man who transformed into Superman when danger was present, Herbert Bagwell was a seemingly normal violin instructor who conjured a troupe of "gypsies" to save the day. Instead of fighting crime, Bagwell's gypsies combated America's disheartening loss of interest in violin music during the 1940s and 1950s.

Bagwell's mission began in 1929, at age 19, when he began teaching violin at Oklahoma City University where he taught for 52 years. His first major project at the university was to organize a string orchestra. Starting with only six players, the group grew to one of the largest in the state During the 1930s and early 1940s.

Despite Bagwell's efforts, the number of string players nationwide continued to fall. The marching band was in its prime as people refused to spend time or effort learning a string instrument. The shortage threatened to silence some of our nation's greatest orchestras, causing even top music schools like Julliard to admit, "Strings are weak."[1]

Herbert Bagwell came to the rescue. In the early 1940s, as an experimental way to generate interest in the string instruments, Bagwell organized a gypsy band. The group, composed of Bagwell's friends and fellow string players, performed concerts for local school children.

These concerts, however, were not the sophisticated, classical style often associated with string instrumentalists. Instead, their music ranged from gypsy stylings to American hits, Latin dance melodies, and classics.

Their appearance was anything but uniform. The group dressed themselves in flowing gypsy attire, complete with glass beads, sashes, and hair coverings. The gypsies played music from memory without a conductor, enabling them to roam through their audience.

As word spread of this gypsy band, invitations to play at schools, festivals, and conventions poured in from across the state. Bagwell's dream was being realized—interest in string instruments was rising!

When World War II began, the gypsies disbanded. Bagwell left his teaching position at the university temporarily to serve in

Bagwell's gypsies charmed audiences around the state and nation with their dancing and their stringed instruments.

the armed forces. Upon his return in 1946 the gypsies again embarked on their mission.

Clothed in more spectacular costumes than before, satin with velvet trim and thousands of sequins, the gypsies' fame continued to grow. Tours stretched nationwide, covering 30 different states. In the summer of 1950, they completed a tour of more than 16,000 miles.

The popularity of the group was not all that continued to skyrocket. In 1946, an estimated 80 school students were studying the violin. In 1950, that number jumped to 500. In the October 20, 1950, edition of *The Advertiser*, Bagwell is quoted as having said, "I am sure that the gypsies have had a lot to do with stimulating that interest."[2]

Bagwell's ingenious idea for a gypsy band possibly resulted from a childhood memory. His father owned the Busy Bee Café in Billings, Oklahoma, where Bagwell spent the earliest years of his life. Bagwell remembers the café served hot cakes and bacon to eastern European gypsies who worked in the oil fields. He claims their music was in his roots.[3]

When the gypsy band held its final performance is uncertain, just as it is impossible to guess how many lives they touched, but one thing remains indisputable. Herbert Bagwell was a superman who, with ingenuity and a touch of glamour, generated interest in a waning art. His passion for the violin was evident in his teachings and travel. Perhaps he explained this best himself by saying, "The violin is popular with human beings all over because it touches your heart."[4]

[1] Aline J. Treanor, "OCU Challenging 'Strings' Shortage," *The Daily Oklahoman*, 18 Nov. 1956.
[2] Macklin, Marguerite, "Herbert Bagwell-Violin Teacher and Leader of a Gypsy Band," *The Advertiser*, 20 Oct. 1950, 1.
[3] Aline J. Treanor, "OCU Challenging 'Strings' Shortage," *The Daily Oklahoman*, 18 Nov. 1956, 2.
[4] Robert Medley, "Violins Touch His Heart," *The Daily Oklahoman*, 27 Jan. 1993, 1, 2.

Herbert Bagwell as he appeared during his time in service to the United States military during World War II.

The C. Q. Smith Student-Faculty-Center was an important part of the university campus beginning in the early 1950s.

completion, the central heating building had been finished, and work was progressing on the student center.[29]

December, 1954 brought a series of television programs to the School of Music. The programs were entitled, "The Musician's Workshop," and aired on Saturdays at 1:30 p.m. Oklahoma City University's musicians alternated weekly with those from Oklahoma College for Women to present the program through the spring semester. The goals of the program were to entertain non-musicians and to help high school musicians prepare for spring music contests.[30]

At the end of December, only the student center remained incomplete in the university's rebuilding program following the fire.[31] Students and faculty played an important role in the center's completion. Although it was opened in March, chairs, lamps, tables, and other finishing touches were still being made in April. Ed Walter, assistant art professor, made all the lamps and ashtrays in the building, and the upholstering department, led by Uville Ogle, worked to finish 100 chairs. The university's building crew was also set to the task of building and refinishing furniture.[32]

Regarding the fire, students reported, "This challenge was met, and in less than a year three new buildings have replaced those destroyed. Today a new Student Center and Book Store, a new Industrial Arts building and a modern heating plant have shown that OCU can meet any disaster and triumph."[33]

In May, 1955, the board of trustees met and created the position of chancellor to be taken by Dr. C. Q. Smith as soon as a successor was found for the position of president. Smith believed this new position would free him of certain administrative duties to allow him to focus on directing the university's development program. The board also officially named two of the new buildings. The student-faculty center was named the C. Q. Smith Student-Faculty Center and the industrial arts building added Loeffler to its name.[34] A formal opening and consecration of the three new buildings was held on May 25, 1955, and drew about 1,000 participants. President Smith and Bishop W. Angie Smith presided over the ceremonies. Mr. and Mrs. Frank X. Loeffler were special guests for the event. A portrait of President Smith donated by W. P. "Bill" Atkinson, former faculty member, was also presented at the ceremonies.[35]

While these buildings were going up on campus, another rebuilding project took place within the athletics department. The Chiefs baseball team won only four games in their first two years since becoming a varsity team.[36] The 1954-1955 season, however, brought the baseball team more victories. The team consisted of students who played baseball not for scholarships or financial assistance, but because they enjoyed the game. The university was proud of the team's growing respect among opposing college teams.[37] At the end of the school year, Abe Lemons was named head basketball coach for the Chiefs after five years as assistant.[38] Paul Hansen was named assistant coach.[39]

For the ninth consecutive semester, *The Campus* won All-American Ratings, the highest award given to a student newspaper.[40]

In June, 1955, school officials decided to move the downtown school, except the law school, to the university's main campus at Northwest 24th Street and Blackwelder Avenue.[41]

The 1955-1956 school year brought much excitement and change to campus. That summer the Surrey Singers were first introduced on a tour to promote the premier of the motion picture, *Oklahoma!*[42] The tour took the singers to New York, New York; Chicago, Illinois; Washington D.C.; Cincinnati, Ohio; St. Louis, Missouri; Tulsa, Oklahoma; and back to Oklahoma City. With each stop the theme *"Oklahoma!"* resonated. The group had a chance to sing on Broadway under the marquee for *Oklahoma!* at the Statue of Liberty, atop the Empire State Building, at Rockefeller Center, and in the lobbies of the Astor and Waldorf Astoria hotels. Their appearance at a salute to Rodgers and Hammerstein at Central Park Mall, however, was the highlight of their trip. They had the honor to perform before many dignitaries associated with *Oklahoma!* dressed in 1890s costumes and dancing and singing for television and live audiences. They were featured on *Merry Mailman, Jinx's Diary,* and *Strike It Rich.*[43]

Oklahoma City University Integrates

Mrs. Jennie Pollard enrolled as the first black student at Oklahoma City University after a unanimous decision by the board of trustees to allow integration of the university. Pollard, who already had bachelor of arts and master of arts degrees began attending the university to study geography and algebra to get her elementary teaching certificate. Five other African-American teaching students enrolled after Pollard, and school got off to a busy start once again.[44]

The last Greek social organization on campus to become nationally affiliated, Phi Delta, was accepted as the 80th chapter of Alpha Chi Omega, national social fraternity for women, and was installed during October, 1955. The oldest of the Greek organizations on campus, Phi Delta was founded at Epworth University, May 1, 1907, and followed the university through its stages as Oklahoma Methodist University and Oklahoma City College.[45]

Pioneers Come in Pairs
Oklahoma City University Integrates

Contributed By Dustin R. Murer

On July 15, 1955, a mother and her daughter began their walk into Oklahoma history as the first of their race to be allowed to enroll at Oklahoma City University. Jennie Pollard enrolled at the university to obtain her permanent elementary teaching certificate. She already held a Bachelor of Arts and a Master of Arts from Oklahoma's only African American institution, Langston University, where she had also worked as a college professor.[1] Her daughter, Patricia, enrolled right after her. After many years of persistence, Jennie and Patricia Pollard were allowed to live Martin Luther King Jr's dream of being judged by the content of their character and not by the color of their skin.

Brown v. Board of Education had finally put the practice of separate but equal to rest in 1954, and a huge battle in the fight for equal rights was won. To adhere to the law, university President C. Q. Smith and the Methodist School Board, headed by Bishop W. Angie Smith, finally approved the integration of the university; Jennie broke the racial barrier on July 15, 1955, as she enrolled for the second summer session to complete her Oklahoma teaching certification.[2] Oklahoma City University was one of the last universities to adopt an integration

Mother and daughter Jennie and Patricia Pollard were two of Oklahoma City University's early African-American graduates. Although neither of their matriculation cards ask the applicant to indicate race only a year later race was a required specification on the application for graduation, an example of this is shown on the card of Alan S. Greenspan.

policy after eighteen of Oklahoma's colleges and universities supported integration.[3] Trying to soften the harsh reality President C. Q. Smith stated:

> There has never been any denominational discrimination at Oklahoma City University. While OCU is the property of the Methodist church all people have been admitted on equal recognition and privileges, irrespective of denomination, affiliation or whether they belonged to a church. We welcomed and invited all to OCU and make no apologies for insisting on a Christian education.[4]

Nonetheless, Smith later felt it was necessary to add that there was no pressure from the community to integrate immediately and there were "certain misunderstandings."[5]

During 1955, Oklahoma's tax supported schools already were on track, and University of Oklahoma and Oklahoma State University were fully integrated. Beginning in June, the University of Tulsa began to rapidly move toward integration to follow suit with publicly funded universities, leaving Oklahoma City University, Oklahoma Baptist University, and Bethany Penicl College the last in Oklahoma to accept integration policies.[6] Since all three were private institutions, they were not directly affected by the threat of losing funds by ignoring the *Brown v. Board of Education* decision, although the law applied to the private education sector also. These institutions announced that their racial policies would end as quickly as possible.[7]

Like the pioneers of the west, Jennie and Patricia Pollard were the first to travel into uncharted territory. They were the first of their race to create a path in a wild wilderness of turmoil for all African Americans to have the opportunity to study at Oklahoma City University. The Pollards came to the university to explore the true boundaries of freedom. They are pioneers for their courage to take the first step into a new world of equality and liberty, things that were withheld for generations.

[1] "Mother, Daughter are First Negroes to Enroll at OCU," *News-Star*, 15 July, 1955, 1A+.

[2] "First Negro Enrolls at OCU," *Oklahoma City University Bulletin*, July 1955, 1+.

[3] "Racial Curb Is Still On," *Democrat*, 8 June, 1955, 1A+.

[4] "First Negro Enrolls at OCU," *Oklahoma City University Bulletin*, July 1955, 1+.

[5] "July 15 Begins OCU Racial Integration," *Capitol Hill Beacon*, 14 July, 1955, 1A+.

[6] "Other Universities Move Rapidly to Join Integration," *Daily Phoenix*, 8 June, 1955, 1A+.

[7] Ibid.

Dorms appeared on campus almost overnight. Smith believed that dormotories were a vital part of the campus experience. Below, clockwise: Smith and Banning halls in winter; Harris Hall; Smith and Banning Halls in spring time; Draper Hall.

September found the Surrey Singers traveling again, this time to the west coast, taking their voices to Hollywood. They sang in an *Oklahoma!* song fest from the Hollywood Bowl, a televised event, as well as brief songfests en route to and from Hollywood.[46]

The geology department celebrated its own work with the display of the tusk of what appeared to be the prehistoric wooly mammoth or mastodon. Bill Whitfield, a senior, had assisted in the excavation of the tusk, and Professor Jack Blythe, head of the Oklahoma City University geology department, identified the discovery.[47] With all of the success the university had obtained, the board of trustees continued to look for ways to build the university. In October, a three and a half million dollar advancement program was approved by the trustees to build dormitories, a fieldhouse, and a pan-hellenic hall, as well as to raise teacher salaries.[48]

In August, 1956, the Surrey Singers again went on the road, this time to Dallas, Texas, and the National Law Convention, appearing with the stars that performed in the movie version of *Oklahoma!*[49] With September came the Methodist Church's observance for Oklahoma City University. In conjunction with this event, the university challenged the church to match a $250,000 gift from V. V. Harris, who required the gift be matched before it could be used. Also in the fall of 1956, an Oklahoma City University student was named Miss Oklahoma. LaDonna Kramer represented the university and the state at the Miss America competition, with the titles of 1954 Keshena Beauty, 1956 Oklahoma Maid of Cotton, and 1956 OCU Basketball Queen already in hand.

The sale of the Rice House to the Kappa Alpha Fraternity marked the passing of an era.[50] The Rice House over the years had served as a home for approximately 850 young men. Delta Psi Omega - which became Kappa Alpha - eventually took over the house, buying it in December, 1956.

Christmas brought an addition to the C. Q. Smith Student-Faculty Center of a Kiva room in the basement for students to relax with games and music.[51] The sororities found a new home soon after the Kappa Alphas became permanent residents of the Rice House. The Josephine Bell Pan-Hellenic Hall was dedicated on February 24, 1957, for use by the three sororities on campus. The hall was named after the university's dean of women by a vote of the Pan-Hellenic Council. The hall afforded each sorority a separate apartment for meetings and other activities.[52] One of the first graduates of Epworth University in 1907, Rev. Q. W. Brakebill, was honored as a guest during the spring commencement exercises.[53] Work began on four new dormitories scheduled to be completed in 1958,[54] and plans were made for Smith's transition from president of Oklahoma City University to chancellor.

Wilkes

Dr. Jack Stauffer Wilkes became president on July 1, 1957. He was described by students as, "A young and a friendly man, a man who does not shirk responsibility and creates a feeling of pride and willingness to cooperate in his co-workers."[55] Wilkes, an ordained minister, began his presidency focusing on the Christian institution's duties to its students. He emphasized the importance of guiding students in choosing the values they would live by.[56]

The 1957 school year brought the 50th anniversary of *The Campus* student newspaper. The newspaper had retained its name as the university changed hands several times, and received honors on many occasions.[57]

The launch of the first man-made satellite, Sputnik, by the Soviet Union brought change and uncertainty both to the university and to the United States. The nation met the Soviet innovation its own satellite program known as the Vanguard project, headed by Commander Jay Smith, a university alumnus.[58]

Spring, 1958, brought the inauguration of Wilkes and the second annual Alumni Day on March 6th and 7th.[59] The day began with a free pancake breakfast for alumni. Five Methodist bishops took part in the official ceremony, and the university key and seal were presented to the president following the keynote speech by Dr. Willis M. Tate, president of Southern Methodist University.[60]

Smith worked hard as chancellor of the university. He focused on raising $10,000 each month toward the principle on debt accrued by the university for building projects,

Basketball grew in popularity during the 1950s as Oklahoma City University changed its mascot from the Goldbugs to the Chiefs. During this decade the Chiefs gained a winning reputation among Oklahoma universities and were often a contender in the state championship.

including the completion of the four dormitories begun in 1957. He started writing a history of the university, as well as preaching, lecturing, and promoting the institution.[61]

The summer of 1958 brought the promise of a new fieldhouse for the athletics program. Although plans had previously been approved for a new practice gym, a fieldhouse offered a more practical solution, offering a building that would seat 3,500 people and be named after George Frederickson, trustee and supporter of the Chiefs.[62] The four new dormitories, Banning Hall, Bess Owen Smith Hall, Stanley C. Draper Hall, and Vernon V. Harris Hall, provided living space for 248 men and 168 women.[63] Also added to the university was a fountain in the campus main quadrangle with a pedestal reserved for a sculpture by Leonard McMurray.[64]

The technical training school, founded in 1950, was busier than ever in 1958. In 1954 it had been renamed the School of Industrial Arts, when students became subject to university requirements and could receive a Bachelor of Arts in industrial arts. Significant changes in the school's curriculum necessitated two more name changes before the name School of Engineering and Industrial Technology was settled on in 1958. Courses offered included aircraft, drafting and design, and refrigeration and air conditioning. Most of the course work offered was at the engineering or semi-engineering level.[65]

The basketball season was good for the Chiefs, with 20 wins and only 6 losses. Two-thirds of the way through the term, the team moved to their new facility, the George Frederickson Fieldhouse.[66]

Two organizations expanded to include new activities and fill new university needs. Out of university tradition and a desire to serve, The Scarabs arose. This organization, named for the Goldbugs of earlier years of the university, served as a liaison between the administration and students. The students engaged in service to the university through a number of projects, including fund-raising for a chapel building on campus, resuming the tradition of lighting the tower in the administration building after every Chiefs basketball victory, planning a revised freshman orientation, and providing the university with informed and enthusiastic student leaders.[67] New to the Methodist Student Movement in 1959 was the Creative Movement Choir, a group of girls who used movement as an expression of worship. They performed for student worship services, churches, and conferences throughout the year.[68]

In September, 1959, a long-awaited addition to campus was completed. A statue named *The Eternal Challenge* was erected at the center of the fountain on the main quadrangle. The monument, a gift from Mr. and Mrs. Erick Lippert, depicted two college students, a female holding a book, and a male holding the "lamp of learning." Two students, Gary and Judie Gardner, modeled for the project.[69]

A brave new world. Top row, from left: Graduation on the Quadrangle; the University Choir. Middle row, from left: The Wooten Observatory which housed the Chamberlin Telescope; members of the Kappa Alpha Fraternity lead a motorcade welcoming home Miss America Jane Jayroe. Bottom row, from left: A student lights the *Eternal Challenge*; young men work on an automobile as a part of the Industrial Arts Program; 1960s aerial view of Oklahoma City University.

NEW

Chapter Six

Partnership

1960

The 1960s welcomed a decade of change. The nation was invested in a largely unpopular war in Vietnam, and young people struggled to define their generation and impact the world in a postive way.

In this decade of turbulance, Oklahoma City University changed with the times with curriculum focused more on the sciences, watching as a man walked on the moon for the first time. The new focus on science not only altered curriculum, but forged a partnership with a prestigious, East coast university known as the Great Plan.

Through the shifting winds of change, Oklahoma City University celebrated the crowning of its first Miss America, Jane Jayroe, an Alpha Chi Omega from Laverne, Oklahoma. Jayroe served not only as an ambassador for a divided nation, but for the university as well.

The campus also acquired two new pieces of sculpture, the *Pioneer Preacher* and *The Eternal Challenge*. The figures depicted in *The Eternal Challenge* were couple Gary and Judie Gardner.

As Oklahoma City University navigated the tumultuous waters of the sixties the institution grew and rediscovered its true identity. Students learned more about who they were as a generation and the university found its place in the community as an innovative, stabilizing university.

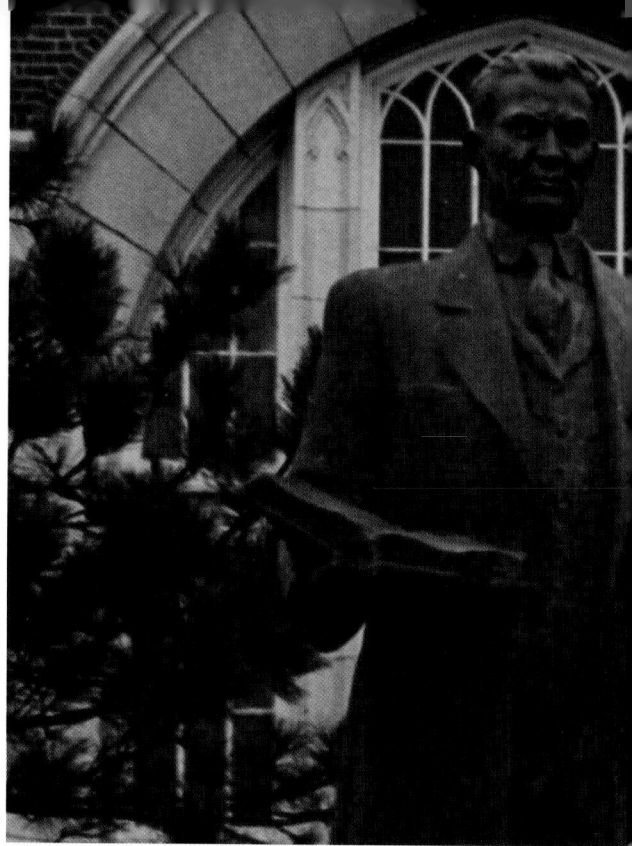

The Great Plan

The lamp of learning burned brightly among the students and administration of 1960. A program known as The Great Plan was dedicated to the improvement of the quality of education at Oklahoma City University. Under this plan, the university partnered with the Massachusetts Institute of Technology (MIT) to plan courses in the fields of physics, chemistry, biology, mathematics, and modern languages. The first courses under the plan were offered in the fall of 1960. A committee of MIT faculty advised the program, making their first visit to Oklahoma City on March 25, 1960.[1] The program was a part of the national focus on science and education in response to the launch of the Soviet Union's *Sputnik.*

To implement The Great Plan, Oklahoma City business leaders began a campaign to raise $2,545,000 for endowed professorships, advanced faculty study, new science laboratories, equipment, and a science library. A scholarship program was also planned to assist able students in attending the university.[2]

The 1960 commencement was accompanied with the unveiling of another statue for the campus, *The Pioneer Preacher.* This statue was created by Bonnie Hicks Doering as a tribute to her father, Reverend Price Beauregard Hicks.[3] Doering, a widely known artist, designed the statue in Italy in 1951 and donated it to the university in 1960.[4] Doering was not the only important figure on campus during commencement in 1960. Senator Lyndon B. Johnson, Democratic Senator of Texas, gave the commencement speech and was awarded an Honorary Doctorate of Humane Letters during the ceremony.[5] Not long after his visit, Johnson was elected Vice President of the United States with John F. Kennedy as the Presidential Elect.

In the fall of 1960, the law school was accredited by the American Bar Association as the university gained stature and acclaim, and world renowned figures visited, Chancellor C. Q. Smith retired.[6]

Four Great Plan classes enriched the education of forty-one freshman students who were admitted into the program that fall. Twenty of these students received Great Plan Scholarships based on their class rankings and intentions to study science, math, humanities, social science, modern

languages, or education. The enriched courses in physics, mathematics, modern languages, and English were available only to students who met the program requirements.[7] In spring, 1961, with Great Plan funds, Oklahoma City University obtained a fully operational language laboratory that allowed faculty to teach more than one language at a time. It also allowed students to compare their pronunciations with those of a native speaker recorded on tape.[8]

While The Great Plan afforded students new opportunities on campus the School of Law was also creating new ways for students to connect with other members of their future profession, when, December 16, the oldest of all Greek letter professional fraternities became part of the school's life. Twenty-five students and twenty-four alumni were initiated as charter members of Phi Delta Phi.[9]

Meanwhile, the Surrey Singers presented their work on an eight week Pacific tour, visiting the armed forces in Japan, Korea, Taiwan, the Philippines, Guam, and Hawaii.[10] The university choir recorded hymns and other music to be aired during the Protestant Hour between July 1 and September 2, 1962.[11]

The MIT advisory committee to the Great Plan returned in November of 1963. They concluded that the base of the Great Plan had been developed and that Oklahoma City University was attracting a higher caliber of students than ever before. They said the institution had moved from a part-time campus to a full-time, 24-hour-a-day campus and that eventually it would move to a 7-day-a-week campus. They were pleased with the university's progress and met with administrators, faculty, and students to plan future improvements and discuss potential problems that might result from its rapid growth.[12] A pebble and flagstone plaza graced the front of the administration building in the spring of 1964, blending with traditional campus landmarks including the sundial left by the class of 1925.[13]

On November 22, 1963, the assassination of President Kennedy united Oklahoma City University. A memorial convocation was held for John Fitzgerald Kennedy. Dr. Dolphus Whitten, encouraged students to serve as Kennedy had served.

"We gather here with a variety of emotions. We come with a sense of loss and of grief…We come with a sense of indignation…We come with a sense of appreciation, desiring to pay tribute to this young man who was our leader...Looking beyond the frustrations of this day, we recognize that each of us is called to serve mankind. The battle is not won. The ideals for which President Kennedy fought have not yet been achieved. It is up to us to make sure that these ideals are realized and that the spirit of brotherhood may grow on the earth."[14]

The Olson Years

Dr. John Frederick Olson assumed the office of president on July 1, 1964. Olson had been at Syracuse University as part of the faculty or administration since 1948. When he became the university's president, he had been vice president of Syracuse, executive assistant to its chancellor, and secretary of the executive committee of its board of trustees.[15]

Only a brief reflective pause marked the arrival of the new president before life on campus continued its normal, busy pace. The Surrey Singers were traveling again in the fall of 1964, this time, on a European tour to perform for armed forces in the United Kingdom, France, Germany, and Italy. The Surreys' trip began on November 15, 1964, and ended January 9, 1965.[16] Back at Oklahoma City University, the MRS institute began its first year. Pronounced "missus," the MRS

The MRS program offered women in the 1960s the opportunity to continue their education. As more and more women began to work outside the home, it became necessary for them to possess basic office and work skills.

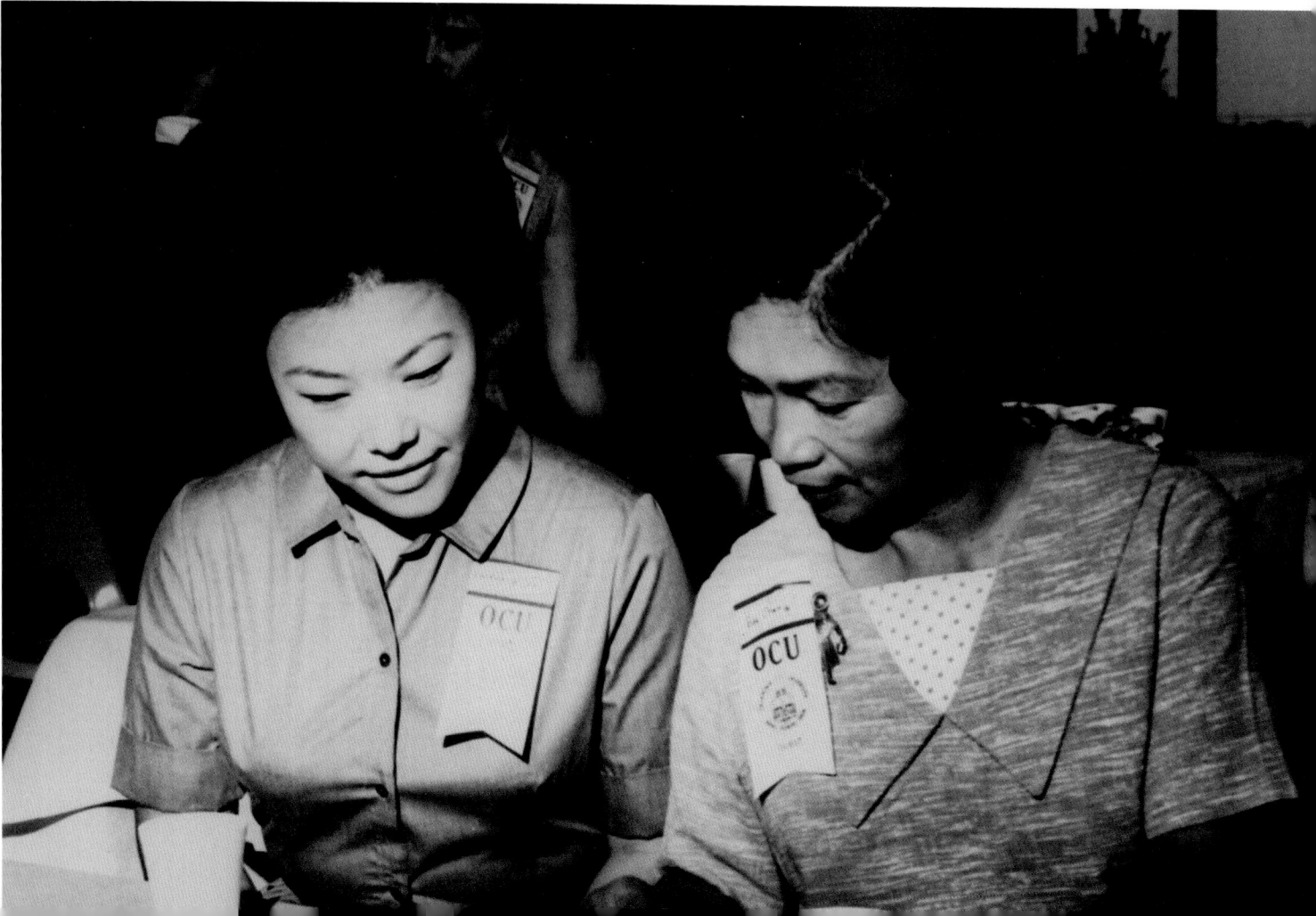

Sculpted to Sculptor
The Eternal Challenge

Contributed By Kali L. Watson

The 1957 school year brought an experience Gary and Judie Gardner would never have imagined. The changes began with an unusual call to the athletics hall for Gary, "It was strange for the coach to call any of us, so I knew something had to be up."[1] Coach Abe Lemons had been contacted by the Chamber of Commerce to see if he could provide a tall, thin boy who would be interested in modeling for a sculpture. Dr. Gardner has always felt Coach Lemons chose him because he had always loved the arts and knew that Gary would actually stay with the project until it was finished. Judie joined the project when Leonard McMurray, the sculptor, asked Gary to find a girl who would be willing to model with him. Of course the logical choice was his girlfriend, Judie Randolph.

Gary was a junior and Judie a sophomore when they began posing for McMurray's sculpture, *The Eternal Challenge*. Gary, a Lambda Chi Alpha and Chiefs basketball player, and Judie, an Alpha Chi Omega member, were both busy and sometimes found it difficult to balance school, practice, Greek life, and work with McMurray. "It was actually quite fun," Dr. Gardner remembered fondly. What he remembered most, however, was that McMurray actually had found a "lamp of knowledge," that he held during their sessions. Although posing was strenuous at times, the project is one of Gardner's most vivid memories from Oklahoma City University.

After the Gardners' marriage in August of 1958 they left the university so Gary could attend dental school at the University of Tennessee. After his graduation in 1962 they returned to Oklahoma where Judie received her master's from the University of Oklahoma and worked as a social worker. The Gardners have two children and, when interviewed, were expecting a second grandchild. Both the Gardners are now retired.

In 1998 the Gardners began a new chapter in their lives. Gary was getting ready to retire from his dental practice and decided to take sculpting lessons. He was just planning on sculpting as a hobby, along with golf. Almost 46 years after being sculpted, Gary has become the sculptor. "I have always been interested in the arts but I think maybe the exposure I gained while working with Leonard McMurray could have a little to do with my new hobby."[2]

In November of 2002 Gardner bid on a project that the City of Lawton was planning. The city wanted a life-sized sculpture of General Henry Ware Lawton, the town's namesake, to present at the town's birthday party in August of 2004. The city chose Gary's bid and he began work on the sculpture in January of 2003. This spurred what will now become an annual project. Because of the exposure he received, Gardner has been commissioned to sculpt an annual award presented by a Lawton social society. The award is the Lawtonian Lifetime Achievement Award. Being chosen to model for a sculpture in 1956 touched the lives of Gary and Judie Gardner in ways than they ever would have imagined.

[1] Gary and Judie Gardner, personal interview, 29 Jan. 2004.
[2] Gary and Judie Gardner, personal interview, 29 Jan. 2004.

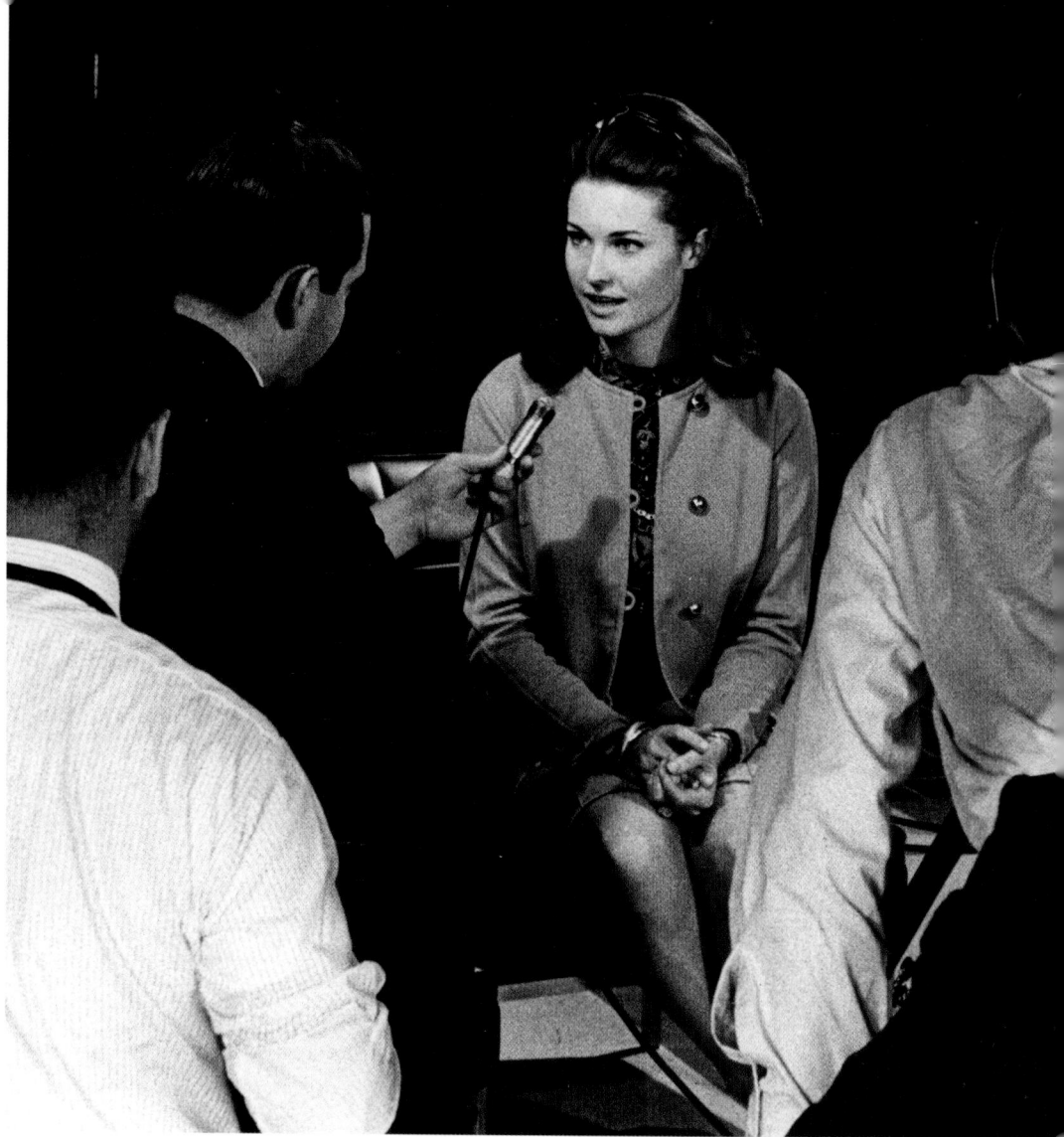

Jane Jayroe, the university's first Miss America spends time talking to the press in the Goldbug Lounge in the C. Q. Smith Student-Faculty Center.

stood for "Mothers Return to School." The purpose of the program was to encourage mature women to further their education in an environment that was not threatening, helping them compete with younger students.[17]

Olson believed great changes were coming to the United States in education, and Oklahoma City University was in a unique situation with an important role to play.

> We are living in the first period of human history wherein it is false to assume that the children's lives will be lived under substantially the same conditions as their parents…Set as it is at the heart of a great urban center it must be an intellectual and spiritual beacon, a guidepost in these turbulent times. O.C.U., as a free-enterprise institution has a special contribution to make to freedom. O.C.U., as a church-related institution, has a special contribution to make to its students and to the culture of our complex nation.[18]

Astronomy students could stand closer to the stars with the addition of the new J. Wooten Observatory and the reconditioning of the six-inch, refractor-type Chamberlain telescope. The observatory was a round, two-story brick building with a wrap-around staircase and a revolving aluminum dome. The telescope, originally given to Fort Worth University by Mr. H. B. Chamberlain in the 1880s, was refinished in stainless steel before being mounted in the observatory.[19]

When President Olson was inaugurated William Pearson Tolley, chancellor of Syracuse University, spoke at the convocation about the type of man needed to run a great university. Bishop W. Angie Smith, in delivering the charge to Olson, said that Olson fit the description of the perfect president as given by Tolley. The stage was set for a new stage of development and the continuation of the Great Plan.[20] Soon after, Olson introduced a $25 million expansion plan for Oklahoma City University as part of his efforts to create an environment where students could grow. His plan included a proposed Bishop W. Angie Smith Chapel, women's and men's dormitories; additions to the power plant, the Fine Arts Building, the C.Q. Smith Student Faculty Center; and a new Great Plan Center, new business school and law buildings, a health center, and a new science center.[21]

Students in the science program during the 1964-1965 school year had to work quickly in the Loeffler Building to keep pace with the rapidly changing world of science. Several research projects were conducted between classes, ranging from a study of sheep hormones to a study of biochemical effects of maintaining rats in the environment used by astronauts in space. In this way students were able to participate in groundbreaking work and learn in a hands-on environment, developing their knowledge in science and also in the methods of research.[22] Journalism students enjoyed classes led by professional journalists, taking tours of newspaper plants, television and radio stations, and public relations offices, as well as receiving on-the-job training through workshops in the different areas of media.[23]

The academic year concluded with commencement exercises that included the first class of forty Master of Business Administration graduates, the first thirty-six law school graduates to receive a Juris Doctorate, and the first fourteen students to earn the Master of Arts in Teaching. Commencement week also brought news to the campus of a generous donation by Mr. and Mrs. John E. Kirkpatrick for an addition to the Fine Arts Building, meeting the need for studios, practice rooms, stagecraft area, dressing rooms, and a 200-seat theater-recital room.[24]

The fall semester was barely underway when Jane Jayroe, a coed from Laverne, Oklahoma, became the first Oklahoma City University student to earn the title of Miss America on Saturday, September 10, 1966. This honor sent Jayroe on a year-long journey throughout the United States and beyond and made her an immediate national celebrity. Jayroe postponed her schooling to fulfill the duties of her title and later returned to complete a Bachelor of Music degree.[25] While Jayroe was away, the campus continued to expand, with work continuing on a new women's dormitory and construction and remodeling continuing on the C. Q. Smith Student-Faculty Center. Expected to begin soon were the improvements to the Fine Arts Building and the construction of the Bishop W. Angie Smith Chapel and Religious Center. On October 22, 1966, Dr. C. Q. Smith, who spent a large part of his life securing buildings on the Oklahoma City University campus, died.

One of the many buildings that Smith had seen completed was Walker Hall, the new women's dormitory. At its opening on September 23, 1967, 252 residents toted boxes up the stairwells and in the elevator. The newly expanded C. Q. Smith Student-Faculty Center had nearly doubled in size. Although part of the addition to the Fine Arts building also was put to use beginning in the fall semester, the full addition would not be complete for several months. The university's first free standing chapel was still being built and expected to be completed sometime in 1968.[26]

When Jayroe returned to school in the fall of 1968 as a junior, she noted how much she had changed through her experience as Miss America. She had traveled more than ever before, seeing not only New York and other great American cities, but also having the opportunity to

Tradition and Community
Greek-Letter Organizations
Contributed By Eric Lee Peeples

The year is 1921. The event is a meeting of the men of the Delta Psi Omega fraternity. "Brother Rutledge brought the Sacred Lantern of Diogenes out of its Royal Cubby Hole, and proceeded to flash its effervescence of illumination on each brother. Having ascertained that each had on the necessary regalia, including the chained pin, set with precious stones roll call by Brother La Fon showed all members present."[1] Later, at a meeting of the women of the Beta Alpha sorority, the members of the sorority gathered in the upstairs room at 320 E. Park Place. "Sister Idabel Morrison carefully pulled down the shades and lighted the seven mystic candles. The meeting was opened in due form, each sister facing the East, sticking her tongue in her left cheek and swatting three times before the scared totem pole."[2]

Throughout Oklahoma City University's history, Greek social organizations have played a vital role on campus and off, affecting those who join the organizations and those who benefit from their many philanthropic activities. Every year, the fraternities and sororities take part in the homecoming celebrations. This helps to bring the campus together and show school pride. The six organizations at the university in 2004 have helped with many philanthropic projects and fundraisers for organizations such as: Habitat for Humanity, the American Heart Association, Campfire for Girls, the Muscular Dystrophy Association, Special Care, a daycare for mentally physically disadvantaged children, Urban Skyline Ministries, and the North American Food Drive. To their members, fraternities and sororities teach leadership skills for use in life after college. Those in Greek organizations consider themselves family, supporting each other through all types of situations. John Warner, a Kappa Sigma said in 1972, "You've always got help when you need it, and you'll always give help when it's asked for. Your greatest advantage here is a brotherhood. A nationwide, lifelong brotherhood." Through the years the Greek social organizations at Oklahoma City University have gone through many changes. However, Greek organizations have continued to help their communities and each other as well as support the mission and goals of Oklahoma City University.

There have been many Greek organizations on the campus of Oklahoma City University over the years.

The sorority Phi Phi Phi, or Tri Phi, had its first ever chapter on the campus of Oklahoma City College in 1923. It was a long-standing joke that the founders of Tri Phi met in a Putnam City beer garden to organize and only intended to select one name for their organization. However, after a few drinks, they saw triple and so chose the same name three times.

Some of the traditions still carried out on campus in 2004 were the athletic competitions between the fraternities. This tradition dates back to 1926 when the Greek men participated in baseball and basketball tournaments. By 2004, football had also become a favorite competitive sport.

The Inter-Fraternity Council and the Pan-Hellenic Council were both founded as the governing bodies for the social fraternities and sororities in 1929 and still function in 2004.

During World War II, the men of Lambda Chi Alpha leased their house to the university because so many of its members had gone to war that at one point, only one active member was on the OCU campus.

In 1942, a new tradition was begun when the first combined function between a fraternity and a sorority took place on campus when the Phi Deltas and Delta Psi Omegas had a Christmas Dance. As of 2004, joint fraternity-sorority functions take place throughout the year.

The gentlemen of the Kappa Alpha Order, who are titled as knights, must stand when a lady enters a room, and try to live up to being a true Southern gentlemen, acquired a cannon in 1958, which they use to fire. As of 2004, however, firing has ceased, and the cannon has become a showpiece, sitting out in front of the fraternity house.

Additional information for this article was taken from: Brill, H. E. Story of Oklahoma City University and Its Predecessors. Oklahoma City: University Press, 1938; Alpha Chi Omega: Opportunities for a Lifetime. 2000. Lifeline Data Centers. 15 Feb. 2004. http://www.alphachiomega.org; Alpha Phi: Delta Delta Chapter. 15 Feb. 2004. http://www.okcu.edu/students/alphaphi/about%20a-phi.htm; Oklahoma City University: Organizations & Clubs. 15 Feb. 2004. http://www.okcu.edu/students; Kappa Alpha Order . . . defining the Gentleman. 15 Feb. 2004. http://www.okcu.edu/students/fraternities; Kappa Sigma. 15 Feb. 2004. http://www.okcu.edu/students/fraternities/kappa_sigma.htm; Lambda Chi Alpha. 15 Feb. 2004 http://www.okcu.edu/students/fraternities/lambda.htm; Coyle, Lee, ed. The Keshena. Vol. 48. Oklahoma City: Semco Color Press, 1952. 88 Vols; Coyle, Lee, ed. The Keshena. Vol. 49. Oklahoma City: Semco Color Press, 88 Vols; Staude, Jennies, ed. The Keshena. Vol. 52. Oklahoma City: Oklahoma City University, 1956. 88 Vols; The Keshena. Vol. 55. Oklahoma City: Oklahoma City University, 1956. 88 Vols; Anderson, Winslow S. Letter to Dr. Eugene M. Antrim, Pres., Oklahoma City University. 7 Apr. 1926; The Scarab. Vol. 21. Oklahoma City: Oklahoma City University, 1943. 24 Vols; Lambert, Arthur R., ed. The Keshena. Vol. 74. Oklahoma City: Oklahoma City University, 1988. 88 Vols; Dobson, Harold L., ed. The Scarab. Vol. 8. Oklahoma City: Oklahoma City University, 1930. 24 Vols; Crabtree, Earl, ed. The Scarab. Vol. 4. Oklahoma City: Oklahoma City University, 1926. 24 Vols; The Scarab. Vol. 7. Oklahoma City: Harlow Publishing Company, 1929. 24 Vols; Mosby, Eunice & Hardy, Dan E., eds. The Scarab. Vol. 19. Times-Journal Publishing Company, 1941. 24 Vols.; The Scarab. Vol. 20. Oklahoma City: Semco Color Press, 1942. 24 Vols; Douglas, Martha & Birge, Jack, eds. The Keshena. Vol. 54. Oklahoma City: Semco Color Press, 1958. 88 Vols; A 1981 Keshena Production. Vol. 67. Marceline: Walsworth Publishing Company, 1981. 88 Vols; Stiles, Stephanie, ed. The Keshena. Vol. 81. 1995. 88 Vols.

[1] The Rambler. Vol. 1. Oklahoma City: Oklahoma City University, 1921. 2 Vols.
[2] Komenski, Deborah, ed. The Keshena. Vol. 1. Oklahoma City: Oklahoma City University, 1972. 88 Vols.

travel in Europe. Her schedule throughout the year had been demanding with engagements almost every night of the week. Although it was exciting, it was somewhat difficult to carry home with her. Jayroe said of her experience,

> If I had to pick out the most important thing I've learned during the year, I think it would be the realization of how very little I do know, how we tend to be content with the narrow limits of our day-to-day experience, and how very much there is to do and to learn. It has been a wonderful year. The crowning of Miss America 1968 in Atlantic City brought the year's reign to a perfect ending.[27]

Oklahoma City University also had changed during Jayroe's year away. The inaugural Mid-Year Institute was held in 1967; this week-long series of sessions with notable visiting speakers took place for many years in early January. Participation was required of all students at least once during their four years of study.

Additional programs were being established and space added to existing buildings, the Kirkpatrick Fine Arts Center was formally dedicated on January 12, 1968, thanks to the generosity of the John E. Kirkpatrick Family. Dr. Capurso, President of Stanislaus State College, presented the dedicatory address and talked about the arts and their important place in the community. Two busts of John and Eleanor Kirkpatrick were permanently displayed in the building, and Mrs. John E. Kirkpatrick was awarded an honorary Doctorate of Humane Letters at the convocation ceremony. The dedication was part of a series of events on campus, including the second annual Mid-Year Institute, which focused on "Man in an Urban Society."[28] The May M. Walker Dormitory was dedicated January 27, 1968, as a memorial to Walker, who partially financed the project.[29]

When the alumni gathered in the C. Q. Smith Student-Faculty center for the 1968 homecoming festivities, they gathered in the Goldbug Lounge, dined in the Scarab Room, and found, enshrined in each area, a molded image of the Goldbug. This renewing of the bond between Oklahoma City University and the Goldbug tradition was to reunite the pre-Chief and post-Goldbug student populations.[30]

In the spring of 1968, colleges and universities all over the nation faced financial crisis, at a time when their public standing was better than ever and they were expanding rapidly. No stranger to financial challenges, Oklahoma City University already had seen that progress only added to the financial turmoil. Contributions grew, but the need for income

The Bishop W. Angie Smith Chapel was the first free-standing chapel erected on the university campus. It was used over the years as a place for weddings, chapel services, and classes.

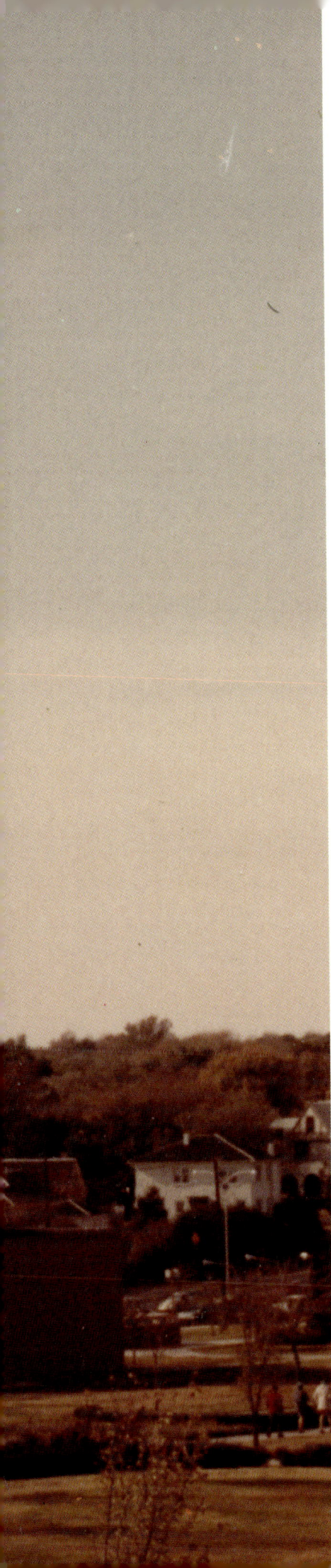

outpaced them. A national report entitled "Editorial Projects for Education" prepared in cooperation with scores of schools, colleges, and universities, emphasized that American colleges were tough enough to endure these problems but, that overall, alumni interest in their alma maters had to grow if universities were to meet the increasing demands of society upon them. The repost stated, "The real crisis will be finding the means of providing the quality, the innovation, the pioneering that the nation needs, if its system of higher education is to meet the demands of the morrow."[31]

The winter of 1968-1969 brought a new dimension of worship to the OCU campus, as Sunday services began in the Bishop W. Angie Smith Chapel. A sixty-voice choir of students under Professor Archie Brown, accompanied by a Holtkamp Organ, were included in worship.[32] Designed by world famous architect Pietro Belluschi the chapel reached heavenward to a height of 151 feet. The main sanctuary seated 650 and a choir of 60.[33] The four stained-glass windows were abstract representations of the four seasons.

Dr. John F. Olson's career at Oklahoma City University ended with a heart attack on June 25, 1969. Students said of Olson:

> He took his duties seriously and pushed himself too hard, working long hours and always taking home a briefcase full of 'homework.'...He brought real communication and participation to the campus community by establishing the Faculty Senate and reorganizing the Student Government...He was a great educator, a fine administrator, a true scholar, a polished speaker, and, above all, a genuine human being.[34]

Acting President Dolphus Whitten, who became president on January 7, 1970, greeted students on the first day of classes and consecrated the grounds dedicated to the construction of a new library on September 11, 1969.[35] He met a campus full of vibrant students who were misunderstood, according to a survey of college students conducted by a national company. While colleges were popularly considered, "hotbed[s] of student discontent and rebellion," the survey showed most students placed emphasis on "improvement rather than upheaval," expressed satisfaction with their college experience, and were optimistic about their futures.[36] About one-third of those surveyed planned to go into the military after graduation, while nearly another third reported they would try to avoid military service. The students also gave no evidence of the supposed "sexual revolution" happening on college campuses, with nearly one-half expressing opposition to pre-marital sex or favoring limitation of sex to the person one expected to marry.[37]

Students, faculty, and concerned citizens interested in examining the war in Vietnam had an opportunity to do so at a rally on the steps of the student-faculty center followed by a prayer service in the chapel, a petition campaign to the community, and a rally for peace at the State Capitol.[38] During this politically charged era, the Student Senate decided to discontinue sponsorship of "honorary representatives of the university," such as the Keshena Kapers Queen, Chieftain, and OCU Princess.[39]

Walker Hall was added to the campus in the 1960s as a part of C. Q. Smith's mission to increase housing for students on campus. The architectural rendition at the right depicts a state-of-the-art new facility.

Dawning of a new age: Top row: Students were concerned about the war efforts in Vietnam throughout the 1960s and 1970s. Middle row, from left: The fountain lighted in front of the Administration Building; inter-fraternal football; Bottom row, from left: Instrumental performance played an important role in the life of the university; vocal music was a significant part of the curriculum during the 1970s as well; the Dulaney-Browne Library was completed early in the decade and served students into the centennial.

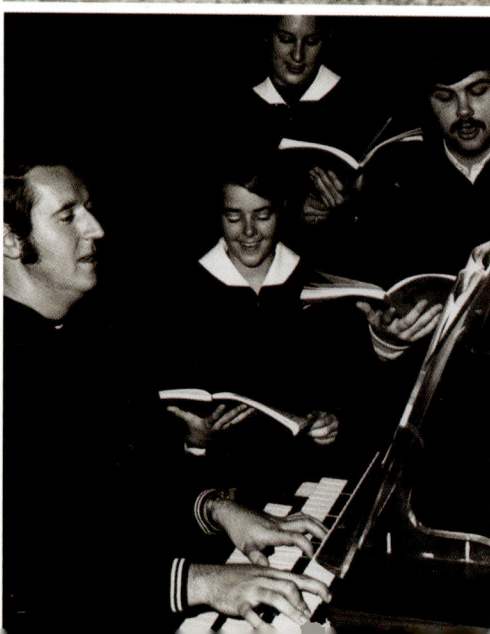

OUT
of the Box

Chapter Seven

1970

Oklahoma City University had many strong programs in the 1970s, and the university offered students many different learning opportunities. Unique programs such as aviation business and the competency-based degree drew students with specific needs and skill bases to the university.

The addition of the Wilson House to campus not only expanded the university grounds but also brought President Whitten and subsequent presidents closer to the campus community. This would prove invaluable in making the president more available and making it easier for the president to share in campus and community events.

The university reached into its community during these years through televised music and dance programs and the community band. In spite of the university's continued prosperity and success in programming and community support, financial struggles once again plagued the university. By 1978, there were rumors that the Methodist institution of higher learning that had been an important part of Oklahoma City for many years would be turned into an office park due to lack of funds. In order to remain competitive in higher education, Oklahoma City University needed enhanced facilities for its students, especially law students. Plans for renovation of the Gold Star Memorial Building into a law school began.

President and Mrs. Dolphus
Whitten dressed in period
clothing rode on a bicycle
built for two.

Dr. Dolphus Whitten

In January of 1970 Whitten was named president of the university. He planned continuation of the Great Plan and the University Studies program designed to provide teaching outside of lectures for the benefit of university students. Whitten answered his appointment with a dedicated reply, "My ambition has never been to hold a title, but to make some significant contribution toward the improvement of higher education." [1]

Incoming students joined the Great Plan through freshman seminars during the winter of 1970. Initiated in 1969, the freshman seminars were part of the new University Studies program. The two-week programs allowed students opportunities outside their traditional program to get to know faculty and to learn about a topic that interested them. No grades or credit were given for the seminars to allow increased flexibility for faculty and students and maximize learning. [2]

Tri-Beta students experienced hands-on learning in a different way during the spring of 1970. Students focused on trying to determine the amount of pollution in the air and water of Oklahoma by taking pollution counts in the surrounding area. [3]

September, 21, 1970, Whitten was the first president to be inaugurated in the Bishop W. Angie Smith Chapel. [4] Across the quadrangle, the six-story Dulaney-Browne Library building was completed and fully furnished. The monumental move of more than 150,000 volumes was completed during the mid-year break between 1970 and 1971 in time for students' return to classes.

Although the addition of buildings and programs, were seen as great strides forward for Oklahoma City University, the institution was in the midst of a financial crisis. With large indebtedness and budget deficits, the university reflected the times as many institutions struggled to meet the demands placed on higher education by students and communities. Oklahoma City University benefited greatly from the strength of the Great Plan and from its relationship with the United Methodist Church. [5] The university had the advantage of unique programs, such as the business aviation program designed by the School of Business in conjunction with Shamrock School of Aeronautics located at Wiley Post Airport in Oklahoma City. Students interested in both fields earned a degree in business administration and became professional qualified aviators. [6]

Innovation in the early seventies seemed incessant as the institution cultivated more unique and defining programs. In 1971 the first dance class was taught on the Oklahoma City University campus. At that time, the dance program was part of the Physical Education department. Ballet Oklahoma used campus facilities, and in turn provided dance instruction. One year later, modern dance became a part of the music department and a performing arts major was offered. [7]

In 1973, the Chiefs received an invitation to participate in the NCAA playoffs, suffering a 103-78 defeat by Arizona State. This marked the eleventh time the Chiefs had made it into the playoffs. [8]

The Wilson House

A president's home was added to campus in 1975. Whitten suggested the idea of the Florence Wilson House when he became president in 1970, because he preferred living close to campus rather than in the home owned by the university

The student body became more diverse during the 1970s and students began to think more individually and question the status quo.

KESHENA 1976 KAPERS

The Wilson House became the home of many Oklahoma City University presidents over the years. Dolphus Whitten and his wife were the first president and first lady to inhabit the on-campus residence.

in Quail Creek. Whitten wanted the university to have more fiscal stability before beginning the project. In 1971 a gift from Wilson, combined with money from the sale of the Quail Creek Home, launched the project. The home was built directly east of the Administration Building, and the Whittens moved in late in July, 1975.[9]

OCU and Aeronautics

An Apollo spacecraft landed on campus in September of 1975, on loan from the National Air and Space Museum of the Smithsonian Institution. The space capsule visit was arranged by an alumnus for the benefit of the students. It was the second Apollo ever flown and the first to reach orbital altitude. It was launched August 25, 1966, from Cape Kennedy, Florida to test the effectiveness of the heat shield used by NASA.[10]

In 1976, the university initiated a pilot program known as the Competency Based Degree Program. The program allowed people to obtain college credit for "college level learning experiences" gained after high school such as civic leadership, on-the-job experience, and community involvement. This program encouraged older people to attend school without having to fulfill all of the degree requirements through classroom work.[11]

Students from the university sang their way into primetime when they were featured in the holiday television special *Sing a Song of Christmas* on December 15th and 25th of 1977. Oklahoma City University and KTVY-TV teamed up to present a special featuring songs and dances by students of the School of Music. Faculty members helped prepare the program and the special was filmed over two days on campus and included the Surrey Singers, Keshena Kids, and brass and woodwind quintets.[12]

Inflation continued to leave most academic institutions in need of a solution to growing financial problems and decreasing enrollment. In December, the administration announced plans to restructure the institution, stabilize financially, and meet changing administrative and academic needs. On January 28, following many hours of budget work, President Whitten

announced an unexpected increase in enrollment for the spring term and the achievement of a balanced budget for the 1977-1978 school year.[13]

The following summer more than seventy musicians participated in the Community Band. The conference, organized on campus by band director Steve Coker, recruited musicians and planned the summer's events. Individuals came from several parts of the state to practice for three consecutive Monday evenings to be ready for the concert on Father's Day, June 18. Some 300 community members gathered in front of the student-faculty center to hear the summer band concert.[14]

1978 brought strengthening of already existing facilities and reorganization to make better use of the existing building space. One of the most important jobs was the remodeling of the Gold Star Memorial Building to meet the needs of a growing population of law students and the requirements of the American Bar Association.[15]

A Visit from a Presidential Hopeful

Former United Nations Ambassador and Central Intelligence Agency Director George H. Bush gave the keynote address for the 13th Annual Mid-Year Institute, which explored the role of big government. The event included films, panel discussions, and question and answer sessions.[16] At the time, Bush was one of the leading Republican contenders for the 1980 presidential campaign.

The renovation of the Gold Star Memorial Building into space for the law school was expected to help retain its accreditation from the American Bar Association.[17]

At a November 13th press conference, President Whitten announced his request to become the chancellor.[18] Whitten noted that, over his twenty-one years in service to the

The Apollo spacecraft visited the campus in September of 1975. The capsule was on loan to the university from the Smithsonian Museum of Air and Space and helped students to better understand the world of aeronautics.

Dr. Leona Mitchell
Alum Makes New York Metropolitan Opera Home

Contributed By Crystal Bell

Fifteen hundred Australians hesitate to blink and part their lips in anticipation as an Oklahoma diva takes their breath away.[1] She performs in the famous Sydney, Australia, Opera House and is more than 8,000 miles from home, but Leona Mitchell's soft spoken persona is nowhere to be found.[2] Her powerful soprano voice is carried to every corner of the theater, and she brings her character, Aida, to life.[3]

How did a small town girl from Enid, Oklahoma, grow up to become a world renowned opera singer? As Rosalyn M. Story stated in her book, *And So I Sing: African-American Divas of Opera and Concert*, Mitchell is one of the busiest singers in the world. It is no secret that a series of events led to Mitchell's undeniable success.[4]

Mitchell's amazing story began in the comfort of her home. She was the tenth child of fifteen. Her father, Hulon Mitchell, was a minister of the Church of God in Christ, and her mother, Pearl Olive Leatherman Mitchell, taught piano and worked as a nurse. All fifteen children sang in their father's choir, and they later formed the Musical Mitchells gospel group. The family choir performed on the radio, television, and even in concert as they traveled Oklahoma.[5] It was not long before Leona's particular gift was discovered, and the young girl was soon singing solos in her father's church.[6]

A high school teacher introduced Mitchell to opera for the first time through a recording. Mitchell said it was "the most wonderful thing [she] had ever heard," and she has been hooked.[7]

Mitchell was the first person to ever receive a full scholarship for majoring in voice at Oklahoma City University, and she performed in ten leading roles by the time of her graduation in 1971. In 1979, she told *Opera News* that she had seen a lot of other singers from other schools and she was grateful for the education she received at Oklahoma City University. After she received her bachelor of arts degree at the university, she continued her education at the Julliard School of Music in New York City.[8]

Not long after graduation, Leona auditioned for the San Francisco Opera. She had won more than thirty vocal competitions by then, and this time was no exception. She walked away with the James H. Schwabacher Award which gave her the opportunity, as a first prize winner, to study under Kurt Herbert Adler, the general director of the San Francisco Opera, for ten weeks. Two years later, Adler employed Mitchell for the first time singing the role of Micaela in the San Francisco spring opera. Mitchell and Adler became friends and would work together many times.[9]

Mitchell went on to become the first native of Oklahoma to sing in the New York City Metropolitan Opera, and she later received several awards for her many accomplishments.

Her hometown recognized the great things she had done and the opportunities she had created for herself. Mitchell was named the "Ambassadress of Enid." Just four years after her graduation from the university, the State of Oklahoma awarded her an "Outstanding Oklahoman" citation, and she received an honorary doctor of music from Oklahoma City University in 1979. In 1983 she served as Ambassador of Goodwill for the Oklahoma Hall of Fame. Mitchell was inducted into the Hall in 2004.[10]

Leona Mitchell accomplished a lot in a very short amount of time. She created a name for herself in a matter of years, but what is more impressive is the longevity of her career. Thirty years later, she is still taking center stage.

[1] Sydney Opera House, 28 Jan. 2004, http://www.touristpublicity.com/html/sydney_opera_house.html.
[2] Ask Jeeves, 28 Jan. 2004, <ask.com>.
[3] Carol Middleton, Conversations with the Black Diva, 2003. 23 Jan. 2004 <http://middlec.customer.netspace.net.au/c_writing/leona.html>.
[4] Kevin S. Hassler, Leona Mitchell, 2001. Biography Resource Center, Gale Group Inc., 23 Jan. 2004, < http://www.africanpubs.com/Apps/bios/1168MitchellLeona.asp>.
[5] Kevin S. Hassler, Leona Mitchell, 2001. Biography Resource Center, Gale Group Inc., 23 Jan. 2004, < http://www.africanpubs.com/Apps/bios/1168MitchellLeona.asp>.
[6] Carol Middleton, Conversations With the Black Diva, 2003. 23 Jan. 2004, <http://middlec.customer.netspace.net.au/c_writing/leona.html>.

[7] Hassler, Leona Mitchell, 2001.
[8] Welcome to Leona Mitchell.com., Norwood Systems Solutions, 20 Jan. 2004, <http://www.leonamitchell.com>.
[9] Hassler, Leona Mitchell, 2001.
[10]Ibid.

Mitchell performed in several Oklahoma City University operas before accepting roles in both San Francisco and New York City.

CIA Director George H. W. Bush spoke on the university campus during the 1979 Mid-Year institute. The Mid-Year Institute was a predecessor to other lecture series such as the Distinguished Speaker Series.

university, he had seen many changes. An institution of a primarily non-resident student body with afternoon classes and no graduate programs had grown into one at which about half of the students were enrolled in graduate and law courses. The academic program had improved, church relations had grown, and the university had worked hard to serve the diverse needs of those in the surrounding community. However, Whitten expressed concern that no long-term fund-raising program had ever been developed, something he hoped to resolve in the position of chancellor.[19]

Walker as President—Focus on the International

Dr. Jerald Walker was chosen to serve in the capacity of president in 1979. An alumnus, Walker began instituting new programs almost immediately. Among the first additions were women's athletics, a new Center for Business and Professional Development, administrative reorganization, the New Era Scholarship, and several fund-raising campaigns. Walker was encouraged by the resolve of the Oklahoma City civic leaders and the United Methodist Church to support the university. His two main goals were to focus on academic quality and community service.

"The best way we can serve the community is to offer quality educational programs that meet the needs of city and state and church. We can offer extra-curricular activities which enrich the quality of life of the city and church, but we're not a 'social agency' in the sense that we provide direct public services. We provide educational opportunities which, in turn, provide the human resources which allow the quality of life to improve," said Dr. Walker. [20]

Law classes were held in the newly renovated Gold Star Memorial Building, making a tremendous difference in student attitudes, according to law faculty. One of the most significant changes was in the law library, which gained approximately 50 percent of usable space, with most going to additional shelving.[21]

Although Whitten had planned to accept the chancellorship of the university, in 1979 he and his wife retired to North Carolina. He wanted to teach classes and relax from the strenuous schedule he kept during his presidency.[22]

On December 8, 1979, a combined celebration of homecoming and the inauguration of Jerald C. Walker as president of the university reunited present and former students with activities that ranged from the Sports Hall of Fame Breakfast to the inaugural ceremony and pep rally in Frederickson Fieldhouse before the evening's homecoming basketball game.[23]

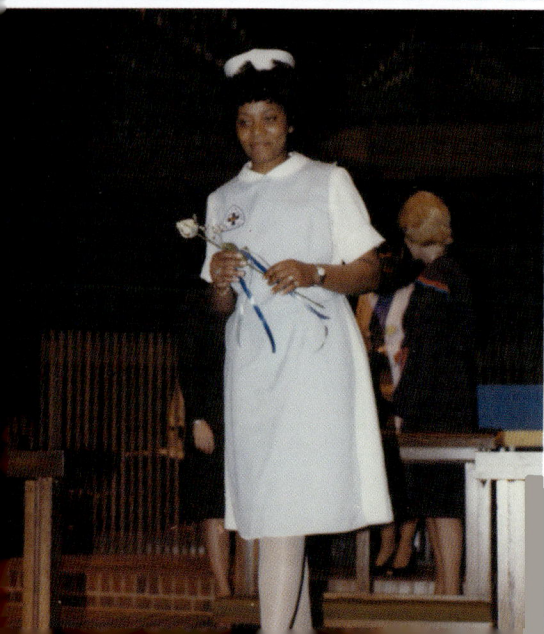

A New Direction: Top row, from left: tennis returned to campus with great success; international students played a larger role on campus and brought many new traditions and customs to the campus community. Middle row, from left: dance became an official part of campus when The American Spirit Dance Company made its home at 23rd and Blackwelder; Susan Powell reigns as Oklahoma City University's second Miss America. Bottom row, from left: the nursing program grows as more students become involved in the health industry and graduated to many prestigious positions in the community.

Chapter Eight

Going International

1980

The 1980s saw the beginning of many new programs on campus directed at meeting the changing needs of a growing population of students. There was a growing need for well-educated students in the fields of computer sciences, nursing, art, dance, and church vocations. Oklahoma City University gladly offered ways for students to either focus in one of these fields or include some education in these areas with other majors.

By 1981, the university was once-again financially stable. Students and community leaders alike invested in Oklahoma City University in the faith that it would continue to provide quality education to its students.

Societies were set up to support some university programs, and First Lady Virginia Walker worked hard to draw well-known performers to the campus for benefit programs. Susan Powell was crowned the university's second Miss America, raising national awareness of the university. The newly-formed Oklahoma Opera and Music Theater Company and the American Spirit Dance Company also drew attention to Oklahoma City University.

With President Walker's commitment to academics came new foundation curriculum that required students to be proficient in certain areas before graduating, with no regard for their chosen field.

The university expanded physically as its programming grew. Many renovations occurred on campus, making facilities more adequate and raising the level of technology available to students and faculty alike. The university had come out of its stupor with gusto.

Students enjoyed relaxing
time on campus between
rigorous studies.

In 1980 Oklahoma City University held its first pow-wow, organized by the Native American Student Association, to bring students together in the spring to celebrate Native American culture and enjoy Native American food.[1]

The School of Law was dedicated April 23, 1981.[2] Also that year, Susan Powell, became the second Oklahoma City University student to win the title of Miss America.[3]

1981 saw the launch of several new programs on campus. As computers became an important part of business and society, computer science was added to available programs. Students could add the emphasis to a degree in business, math, science, humanities, social sciences, or mass communications. Oklahoma City University also teamed with St. Anthony Hospital to launch a joint nursing program to offer a bachelor's degree in nursing. The new program, which would allow students to learn for two years at Oklahoma City University and then receive two years of clinical training at St. Anthony hospital, was expected to begin in the spring of 1982. Beginning in the fall, 1981, semester, art students could concentrate on Native American art.[4] Professor Jo Rowan came to the university to develop a uniquely American dance program. It allowed students to enter career-oriented classes in jazz, tap, and ballet, which would also benefit students interested in musical theatre.[5] The School of Religion and Church Vocations was created, off-campus Master of Business Administration programs were begun, photo-journalism was added to the mass communications department, and the Master of Liberal Arts program became popular.[6]

In the summer of 1981, President Walker reported that Oklahoma City University's finances were in order. The endowment had tripled in the previous 24 months, and the university operated with a balanced budget and a modest surplus during the 1980-1981 fiscal year.[7] In summer 1981, Bob Hope, the university's second Miss America Susan Powell, entertainer Vic Damone, the Preservation Hall Jazz Band, and the Surrey Singers performed to benefit the Oklahoma City University Library Society. A capacity crowd filled the Civic Center Music Hall downtown.[8] The Library Society, formed by the president's wife Virginia "Ginny" Walker, helped provide money for the university's library. Mrs. Walker's personal relationships with performers brought many celebrities to campus during her husband's time as president.[9]

Fencing was a new campus sport in 1981,[10] and enrollment topped 3,000 students for the first time.[11] Susan Powell returned to campus on Friday, October 17, 1981, to be honored in a special presentation. She performed for the audience of students, faculty and friends, joining the Surrey Singers in a song and dance routine.[12]

Dynamite Diva
Kristin Chenoweth, Broadway Star
Contributed By Stephanie D. Joiner

She's a 4'11", squeaky-voiced, blonde powerhouse who lights up a room. She is a daddy's girl, Broadway's dream come true, and heaven to the human ear. She won a Tony Award®, released a solo album, and starred in her own sitcom. A graduate of Oklahoma City University, Kristin Chenoweth is one of the many successful performers who began their careers at the university's performing arts programs.

Chenoweth's mother remembered her singing herself to sleep when she was very little and singing in church. Kristin recalled seeing a ballet on TV and thinking, "I want to do that," when she was only 4 years old. She has been performing ever since.[1] Florence Birdwell, her voice teacher at Oklahoma City University, said Chenoweth knew from the start "how to sing a song." She sang from her soul.

Known as "Kristi" at the university, she was very active in the music school. The *Keshena* yearbooks demonstrate her involvement in Keshena Kids and Surrey Singers during her first few years as a musical theater major. In these two groups, she performed in school shows and functions throughout Oklahoma. After graduating, she earned her master's degree in opera performance. She was in many of the musicals and operas at Oklahoma City University during both her undergraduate and graduate years, including *La Traviata, Annie Get Your Gun, A Little Night Music, Oklahoma!, Guys and Dolls, Die Fledermaus,* and *The Fantasticks*.[2] Chenoweth and Birdwell both recalled her role as "Cunegonde" in *Candide* as one of her greatest accomplishments on campus, and it is a role Chenoweth still loves.[3] Many may also remember her unforgettable performance of "Art is Calling Me," when she won the talent competition and title of Miss OCU in 1991.[4] She went on to win second runner-up at the Miss Oklahoma competition.[5]

Interviewers frequently comment on Chenoweth's height. She once said, "I used to want to be tall, and I thought, 'If I were tall, people would say I was pretty and not cute.' Then I realized there were worse things than being called cute…So I've decided my height ain't so bad."[6] The unique thing about Chenoweth is that many who meet her in person say she is exactly what she seems like from far away: bubbly, talkative, and truthful. Birdwell commented, "She is like a diamond. No matter how small…she is still pure at heart." Her honest, loving nature is consistent onstage and off.

In an interview with Nancy Rosati of the Web page, *Talkin' Broadway*, Chenoweth spoke about her experience after she left Oklahoma City University. She planned to attend Philadelphia's Academy of Vocal Arts on a full scholarship. Deciding that the name "Kristi" was too light for opera, she added the "n". Before she got to Philadelphia, a friend convinced her to audition for a musical called *Animal Crackers*. Kristin got the part and gave up her scholarship to follow her heart to Broadway. Now she is eternally busy in Broadway shows, concerts, TV appearances, and movie shoots. She has been seen in ABC's *The Music Man* and *Annie*, New York's *A New Brain*, *Steel Pier*, *Epic Proportions*, and *You're A Good Man, Charlie Brown* in which she won her Tony Award® for her portrayal of "Sally." She also has a Sony-produced solo album called, *Let Yourself Go*, and starred as Glinda the Good Witch in *Wicked* on Broadway in 2003 and 2004.[7]

In the spring of 2004, Kristin was invited to perform with the New York Philharmonic's concert version of *Candide* playing Cunegonde, a role she played in graduate school.[8] This is just one of the many things she has taken with her from her college experience. Noted Birdwell, "She is the same person now as she was when she was here… She has such honesty, and fame hasn't touched her at all. She never forgets what Oklahoma City University did for her."

[1] "Special Guests for December 14, 2002: Kristin Chenoweth," A Prairie Home Companion, 23 Jan. 2004, http://www.prairiehome.org.

[2] Nancy Rosati, "Spotlight on Kristin Chenoweth," *Talkin Broadway*, 1997-2004, 23 Jan. 2004, http://www.talkinbroadway.com/spot/chenoweth3.html.

[3] Ibid.

[4] Patterson, Andrea, "Senior Chenoweth Crowned Miss OCU," 9 Nov. 1990, *The Campus*, Volume 84, No. 8.

[5] "Biography for Kristin Chenoweth," *Internet Movie Database*, 23 Jan. 2004, http://us.imdb.com/name/nm0155693/bio.

[6] Ibid.

[7] *Kristin Chenoweth*, 2003, 23 Jan. 2004, www.kristincheno weth.com.

[8] Portantiere, Michael, "We Need a Little Kristin," 15 Oct. 2003, *TheatreMania.com*, 23 Jan. 2004, http://www.theatermania.com/content/news.cfm?int_news_id=3983.

Chenoweth starred as Glinda the Good Witch in the Broadway production of *Wicked*. Chenoweth has worked on and off Broadway for many years, starring in her own sitcom and in music theatrer productions.

As Oklahoma City University formed its first offical school of dance, the arts gained more recognition than ever before around Oklahoma City and the campus. Under the leadership of Jo Rowan the American Spirit Dance Company tapped, kicked, and shuffled their way into the hearts of students, faculty, and the community.

Ground was broken for the Noble Center for Competitive Enterprise, and the School of Law, housed in the newly renovated Gold Star Memorial Building, was dedicated.[13] Homecoming 1981 held a different sort of excitement as Oklahoma City University's original mascot, the Goldbug, was unveiled. The mascot did not replace the official Chiefs mascot but was used to strengthen the university's tradition and heritage.[14]

Roy Clark brought his Las Vegas show to the Oklahoma City Civic Center Music Hall during the spring of 1982 as a Library Society benefit. Clark was joined by Will Rogers Jr. and Susan Powell.[15] Beginning in the fall of 1982, the university implemented a new general education program known as the Foundation Curriculum. It was designed to initiate students into disciplines that had proven useful in the individual search for meaning and understanding in life. New courses implemented as part of the program included Interpersonal Communication, Economics and the Quality of Life, Introduction to Biblical Literature, Evolution of Science and Technology, and Mathematics, Models, and Computers.[16] The university developed a new degree in music/business administration for students interested in the growing field of music management.[17]

The Oklahoma Opera and Music Theater Company was formed in 1982 as the university's music theatre and opera productions gained national recognition and respect. This allowed the production of even more professional cultural events for Oklahoma City through the university.[18] While the music school developed a professional company, the art department took on a large project under commission from the Bricktown Development Corporation for several large billboards and murals as part of the renovation of downtown Oklahoma City.[19] The American Spirit Dance Company also was formed under the direction of Jo Rowan and performed in Oklahoma Opera and Music Theater Company productions throughout the year.[20] An English writing center was created for the benefit of all students, who could now receive help with their writing skills for class assignments.[21]

Baseball and tennis players received a new $100,000 Sutton Baseball-Tennis Complex providing two indoor hitting cages, an indoor pitching area, a player locker room-lounge, three coaches' offices, an umpire dressing area, equipment room, shower facilities, and private and public restrooms. The Chiefs men's basketball team found a new home at the State Fair Arena, where they played all 1982-1983 home games.[22] The Lady Chiefs played in the Frederickson Fieldhouse.[23]

The science building received funding for a facelift in the spring of 1983. Dr. Jose Riguel, an Oklahoma businessman and alumnus, made a substantial donation for the renovation of the science building.[24] The holistic approach to healing was a new development in the Oklahoma City University/St. Anthony School of Nursing and in the field of health in the early 1980s. The university was one of the few schools in the country that offered a clinically-oriented holistic nursing degree program in 1983.[25] The School of Law developed a law/theology dual degree program with the cooperation of Phillips University's Graduate Seminary in Enid. The program began in fall 1983.[26] The university was also able to offer students a Doctor of Ministry degree through Southern Methodist University, students working on this degree were taught by professors from both schools and received their degrees from Southern Methodist University.[27] Oklahoma City University was chosen by the United Methodist Church as the fourth national center for minority leadership development within the church. The university would recruit, train, and deploy Native Americans in ministry to strengthen Indian congregations. The university was chosen for this position because of its convenience for Native Americans.[28]

Oklahoma City University began offering an education alternative for people who could not attend night school or college full time. New in the fall of 1983, the Weekend

Soccer became increasingly important in the 1980s as Brian Harvey began a new program for both men and women on the campus.

College included traditional academic courses, personal and professional development classes, microcomputing short courses, and more. One component of the Weekend College was the High School Bridge Program, designed to introduce high school juniors and seniors to the university campus and faculty through non-credit courses in relevant areas such as vocabulary building, writing, decision-making, and career choices.[29]

The School of Management and Business Sciences began holding classes in the newly built Noble Center for Competitive Enterprise during the fall of 1983. The $3.5 million building provided accommodations for the expanding business school: twenty IBM microcomputers were available to students in the computer center, and the building housed the Oklahoma Commerce and Industry Hall of Honor, the Business Research Center, the Center for Business and Professional Development, and the Rowntree Auditorium.[30] Abe Lemons returned to the university after a ten-year-absence to renew his coaching relationship with the Chiefs men's basketball team.[31]

In May, 1984, Oklahoma City University captured its first ever golf championship in the Midwestern City Conference.[32] The Homsey Computerized Legal Research Center opened, President Walker made his first visit to Taiwan to begin "sister college" relationships overseas, and Cary Grant did a benefit for the Opera Society.[33] Ground was broken for the B. C. Clark Memorial Clock Tower, which was completed the next year, and the Gallery Society was founded by Virginia Walker.[34]

During the spring of 1985, the School of Management and Business Sciences began offering a joint degree program in business administration and Asian studies to train students in Asian and American business practices. Sister relations with two colleges in Taiwan and one in Korea allowed student exchanges, scholarships, faculty exchanges, and joint degree programs between participating institutions. By spring, 1985, more than 100 Asian students had enrolled in both undergraduate and graduate degree programs at Oklahoma City University and in the Master of Business Administration (M.B.A.) programs in Japan.[35] By the end of 1985, Oklahoma City University offered classes in Hong Kong, Singapore, Malaysia, and Taiwan.[36] The university also signed an agreement to teach a two-year M.B.A. program, in Tianjin, People's Republic of China.[37]

The Chiefs softball team finished the 1984-1985 season 25-32 with the highest number of wins in its history and its first tournament win, taking NCAA Mid-West Region.[38]

Marie Osmond, the Osmond Brothers, and Vic Damone performed at the 1985 Library Society benefit.[39] That summer, President Walker's book, *The

State of Sequoyah, became available. Proceeds from its sales were donated to the university's scholarship fund.[40] The university continued to strive to keep close ties with the United Methodist Church. The university staff and students regularly gave time to local churches, preaching, teaching, and serving.[41]

The university's B. D. Eddie Business Research and Consulting Center received Small Business Institute designation in 1986. The research center had the responsibility of providing accurate, useful information to its clients and helping to solve various management problems. Teams of business students led by a graduate student learned about business and worked through the center for class credit, meeting professional standards, and consulting with businesses.[42] M.B.A. classes began in China in January, 1986, when Dr. Fitzgerald spent 31 days in Tianjin teaching Financial Planning and Control and International Finance.[43] The Chiefs softball team ended the 1985-1986 season only one game away from a National Association of Intercollegiate Athletes (N.A.I.A.) national championship.[44]

Bill Cosby performed a benefit for the Library, Gallery, and Opera Societies in 1986.[45] During matriculation convocation in the fall, the College of Performing Arts was officially named for Margaret E. Petree in appreciation for her commitment to the university.[46] When classes began in the fall, soccer was a new sport on the campus, headed by Coach Brian Harvey.[47]

Facing page: Oklahoma City University softball teams enjoyed many victories as athletics became a more central part of the campus community. Below: Susan Powell, Oklahoma City University's second Miss America, performed on stage in the Kirkpatrick Auditorium.

The collapse of the Oklahoma City-based Penn Square Bank was a topic of local and national interest in the spring of 1987. One course titled, "The Rise and Fall of Banking in Oklahoma," was offered as a Master of Liberal Arts class, allowing students to explore the banking regulations, banking trends, and the variables that affected Penn Square Bank and sparked a national financial crisis.[48]

In 1987, the School of Nursing received the highest accreditation allowed by the National League of Nursing, and the dance and arts management programs continued to soar under the leadership of John Bedford and Jo Rowan. The American Spirit Dance Company's annual show had become a huge success, and the members performed regularly at Oklahoma City arts events, benefits, and out-of-town shows.[49] The Chiefs men's basketball team finished a record-breaking season, compiling 34 consecutive victories before losing in the second round of the NAIA national tournament.[50] President Walker began a program with the Police Administration of the People's Republic of China to train professional police in criminal justice, police administration, information systems management, and educational administration.[51] The Kiva in the student-faculty center was transformed in 1987 into Alvin's Café, named after Alvin Naifeh.

1988 brought a new title to the Lady Chiefs: NAIA National Basketball Champions. The Goldbug Building, which had fallen into disrepair, was demolished. The Dawson-Loeffler Science and Mathematics Center was re-opened after a $1 million renovation, and a new graduate degree in computer science began. Jill St. John performed on campus to benefit the Opera Society. The School of Religion and Church Vocations was renamed the Wimberly School of Religion in

Facing page: Dancers worked for countless hours to refine their craft, often foregoing other campus activities in order to rehearse. Below: Jo Rowan demonstrates a portion of a routine for a studio filled with eager dance students.

Left: Ground was broken for the B. C. Clark Memorial Clock Tower in 1984. The clock would stand as the campus' only significant timepiece for years to come. Chimes would be added in 2003 and dedicated during the annual Light the Campus Celebration. Right: The Surrey Singers played an important role in the history of the university. They are seen here in the early 1980s.

honor of Owen and Vivian Wimberly, who established and endowed a professorship and an endowed religion scholarship,[52] and the School of Business was renamed the Meinders School of Business to honor Herman Meinders and his wife LaDonna Kramer Meinders for their commitment to the university.[53]

In 1989, AT&T announced plans to make Oklahoma City University the "Campus of Tomorrow," and Multimedia Cablevision announced an agreement to provide the university with its own television station to be used for educational and cultural programming. AT&T planned to install a digital communications system that would allow personal computers in residence hall rooms and all offices. The focus of the project was a centralized telephone system featuring voicemail.[54] The Clara E. Jones Rowntree Administration Building was also officially named.[55] Since 1979, the university's momentum had been outstanding, with an increase of 541 percent in endowment, 218 percent in assets, 450 percent in gift income, and 39 percent in enrollment.[56]

President Walker asked a master wood craftsman and retired Methodist minister, Bonner Teeter, to create a mace as a symbol of the university presidency, and, he finished it in 1989. The

wood mace incorporated as symbols a globe, the Bible, a cross, a wigwam, and a peace pipe.[57] During the winter of 1989, construction was underway on the new Petree College of Arts and Sciences building, which replaced the old brick-veneered Army barracks structure that had housed arts and sciences classes.[58] Groundwork was laid for the establishment of the Soviet Executive Development Program. The first American university to offer this program, Oklahoma City University received its first class of 22 Soviet aviation industry officials on September 10th for a business management course. On September 23rd, the first Soviet-American educational joint venture was signed between the USSR's Institute of Economics of the Academy of Sciences, Enterprise Fenix, and the university.[59]

Ninety years of excellence: Top row, from left: The Sarkeys Law Center is completed on campus; the adminstration building still continues to be an important part of campus. Middle row: Miss America, Shawntel Smith. Bottom row, from left: Walker displays the men's Basketball trophy; Kamp's Grocery store plays a role in university life; Herman Meinders unveils Morrison Tucker's plaque at the Tucker Hall Dedication.

Students learned through hands-on experience in the 1990s by producing KOCU-TV and tutoring their peers in the learning enhancement center. Oklahoma City University continued to provide high-quality private education to students and to serve the community. As an outstanding Methodist university, the university had the opportunity to mentor other universities and to continue developing specialized programs for its students. The university also participated in the education of the community through programs like the ASTEC space camps.

Oklahoma City University's sports programs continued to grow and succeed as the men's athletics program achieved high ranking in the NAIA and soccer was added to the varsity sports available to women.

A new school of nursing meant that the university could educate more students to fill the growing need for nurses in Oklahoma. The education of nurses was especially important following the bombing of the Alfred P. Murrah Federal Building in Oklahoma City on April 19, 1995. Relief efforts were carried out by Oklahoma City police officers, rescuers, nurses, doctors, and laymen alike. Many members of the campus community donated their time, expertise, and resources to assist in the recovery effort that left unthinkable destruction.

Shawntel Smith became Oklahoma City University's third Miss America. Walker began his seventeenth year as university president, the longest term in the university's history.

A new athletic logo made the university mascot the star. It was implemented during the 1999-2000 school year.

HOME at the Top

Chapter Nine

1990

Gladys Tucker speaks at the dedication of Tucker Hall, named in honor of her late husband, banker Morrison G. Tucker. The Hall served as a conference room on the main floor of the Meinders School of Business.

Larry Webb became the university's first television station director in April, 1990. Webb was responsible for generating approximately 10 hours of programming a week during the first two months of operations.[1] KOCU-TV went on the air July 25th for the first time. Over time, the programming on this station would increase to twenty hours per week. Mass communications students worked as crew members and assisted with various phases of productions for the station in order to gain experience in the field.[2]

The new $2.5 million Petree College of Arts and Sciences building opened on schedule in the fall of 1990 on the site of the former Rice Kappa Alpha house.[3] Within the arts and sciences building, the writing center became the Carlock Learning Enhancement Center, the new name emphasizing the center's increased services to students.[4]

President Walker announced that Oklahoma City University was selected by the United Methodist Church to assist the Latin American Educational Center in Rosario, Argentina, in developing the Universidad Methodista Argentina, the first Methodist University in Argentina. Beginning in 1991, faculty and staff traveled to Argentina to provide consulting, curriculum, accreditation information, teaching tips, and more.[5] The university also had the opportunity to provide management education to members of the Czech Republic and Slovakia. The university signed an agreement with a major industrial factory to create The Center for Executive Management, an executive development program.[6] In 1991 the Chiefs men's basketball team won the NAIA national championship.[7] That fall international opera star, Chris Merritt, performed a benefit concert in the Kirkpatrick Auditorium on Friday, March 6th for the university's music scholarship funds.[8]

By spring, 1992, airtime was increasing for KOCU-TV, allowing students to get additional hours of hands-on experience.[9] The Chiefs men's basketball team won its second straight NAIA championship. They posted a 38-0 record and set the NAIA record for consecutive wins, 54 wins dating back to the 1990-1991 season.[10] In fall, 1992, the college of Performing Arts dedicated a new recital hall named after Margaret E. Petree. A week of festivities surrounded this gift, including a benefit voice recital by alumna and New York Metropolitan Opera star Leona Mitchell.[11]

Win Case was named Oklahoma City University's men's head basketball coach. Case hoped to continue the tradition of great basketball and joked that he would "be funnier than Abe Lemons, be a better person than Paul Hansen and win more games than Darrel Johnson." [12] The 1991-1992 men's athletics program won second place in the all-sports contest sponsored by the NAIA.[13]

At an anonymous donor's request, the arts and sciences building was named after President Walker, becoming the Walker Center for the Arts and Sciences.[14] Soccer joined the women's athletic's program in the fall of 1993 as the fourth varsity sport offered to female students. Men's soccer coach Brian Harvey became coach of the women's team as well.[15] Construction was underway on the Sarkeys Law Center, in the fall of 1993.[16] Construction on a new School of Nursing building began in March of 1994.[17] The Chiefs men's basketball team captured a third NAIA championship that year and the university became the only institution in the country to ever win three out of four available NAIA national championships.[18]

Aerospace Science and Technology Education (ASTEC) of Oklahoma began as a summer space camp for children in 1986. In 1994, after years of hard work and curriculum planning on the part of the program's founder, Dr. Freda Deskin, it became a nationally recognized instructional model, and NASA began providing training and materials for the teachers of ASTEC. In 1994, it became an official department of the university.[19]

The School of Nursing was ready for classes in August, 1994, and nursing students moved from their previous home at St. Anthony Hospital Building to the on-campus facility. The school was renamed the Kramer School of Nursing after Mr. and Mrs. E. J. Kramer and their daughters, Dr. Ruth Seideman and LaDonna Kramer Meinders.[20]

The 1990s saw the completion of the Kramer School of Nursing. The university's nursing school finally had a permanent home. The building was named in honor of the parents of LaDonna Kramer Meinders.

To honor the late Morrison G. Tucker, the university named the area in the Noble Center for Competitive Enterprise, housing the Oklahoma Commerce and Industry Hall of Honor, the Morrison G. Tucker Hall. Tucker was an Oklahoma City businessman and banker who served on the board of trustees beginning in 1974.[21] In spring, 1995, the university received the largest bequest in its history to that date with the receipt of 87 percent of Margaret. E. Petree's estate valued at $9,325,000. The university also received an original painting by Margaret Petree and a $450,000 check to increase the Petree endowment in the School of Music to $1 million.[22]

On April 19, 1995, the Alfred P. Murrah Federal Building in Oklahoma City was destroyed by a bomb, that killed 168 and damaged at least 100 buildings in the downtown area. Students and professors alike had an opportunity to serve their community. Nursing professors and students immediately responded to deperate requests to any individuals with medical training, with some helping at the site and others at St. Anthony Hospital. The university's entire faculty, staff, and students assisted the Red Cross and other organizations in their relief efforts. The M.B.A. Alumni of Singapore expressed their condolences for the lives lost in the bombing and presented a tree to the university as a living memorial to honor the people of Oklahoma City for their faith and strength in coping with the destruction.[23]

The 1994-1995 the Chiefs men's basketball team won the conference title for the second straight year, the fourth time in five years. Although they did not win the national championship, the team was happy with its season.[24]

The third Oklahoma City University student was crowned Miss America in 1995 and served in that position in 1996. Shawntel Smith returned to campus for a luncheon, presentation, and press conference on October 13, 1995 after her crowning.[25] At that time Oklahoma City University had become the largest private university in Oklahoma with an enrollment of 4,576 students in the fall of 1995, surpassing the University of Tulsa by 200.[26] The Writing Across the Curriculum program was implemented in 1996. Under the program, students were required to learn and practice oral and written communication early in their college careers through the foundation curriculum and throughout all classes.[27]

The Chiefs men's basketball team won an unprecedented fourth NAIA National Championship in 1996,[28] and the OCU softball team won an unprecedented third consecutive national championship.[29] In 1996, Walker began his seventeenth year as president, having occupied the office longer than any person who preceded him.[30]

Fall, 1997, marked the beginning of a new home for campus sororities when ground was broken for the Nellie R. Melton Pan-Hellenic Quadrangle.[31] Roy Clark performed in another benefit concert; his visit kicked off the Roy Clark Endowed Scholarship. He received an Honorary Alumnus Award at a luncheon to recognize his efforts and to support the beginning of the new scholarship.[32]

OCU/ASTEC began planning a new on-campus complex to house the space shuttle, space station, mission control, classrooms, and a theater for the aerospace program. With the generosity of Oklahoma businessman Jackie Cooper, Oklahoma City University obtained the historic Wiley Post hangar for the proposed ASTEC complex.[33]

On October 3, 1997, the board of trustees announced that, after hospitalized on March 26 for a cerebral hemorrhage, President Walker would assume a new position. Although he returned to the president's office in the fall, he continued to undergo therapy, and, after several months, he chose to resign from his post as president and serve as the university chancellor.[34]

Dr. David Cawthon was named interim president while the board searched for a new president. One of Cawthon's first acts as interim president was to thoroughly audit all areas of the university to evaluate it in terms of mission, integrity, and responsibility.[35] The Meinders School of Business was granted professional and national accreditation by the Association of Collegiate Business Schools and Programs (ACBSP) on June 28, 1997. At the time, only 445 business schools in the United States had professional accreditation.[36] In spring, 1998, all five of the university's spring sports qualified for the NAIA Spring Championship games. This marked the second time that all of the spring teams had qualified for the games, with the first qualified in 1992.[37]

Alvin Naifeh
Bringing Joy to Campus for More Than 50 Years
Contributed By Matt Wills

Alvin Naifeh has seen Oklahoma City University change and evolve into a great institution. He has had numerous roles on campus but, most of all, Alvin is known as the man with a smile who will always greet you. He became an official campus celebrity in 1987 when the student café was named "Alvin's" to thank him for his many years of service to the university.

Alvin's decision to attend Oklahoma City University did not provide much of a change in scenery since he only lived a mile away from the campus. Alvin began studying at the university in 1954 as a religion major, and was involved in the campus newspaper and the yearbook. He occasionally acted and worked behind the scenes at Lyric Theater of Oklahoma from 1963 to 1990. He then started working in the campus mailroom and people all over campus enjoyed socializing with Alvin as he delivered their mail. In 2003 he began working at the Henry J. Freede Wellness and Activity Center managing the daily tasks of keeping it open. When asked in an article for *Focus* magazine if he had any plans to retire he replied, "Not if I can help it. I'm not getting older. I'm getting better." [1]

In the hustle and bustle of college life, students and faculty alike sometimes get wrapped up in things and forget about others. No matter how busy Alvin might be, he always takes time out his day to make being friendly a top priority. When students and alumni were asked to submit their favorite memories of Alvin for an article in *Focus*, many stories were submitted, and they all mentioned Alvin's kindness and loving personality. [2]

Alvin is well known for his amazing knowledge of movie trivia. For many it has become a goal to stump Alvin with a question about a movie that was made from the 1940s to the 1970s. That goal has proved to be nearly impossible. Alvin's passion about movies is evident upon setting foot inside his apartment and seeing his vast collection of classic movies and memorabilia. He has attended numerous film conventions and collected multiple autographs.

Just as Alvin has seen the film and television industry evolve, he has seen major physical changes on the OCU campus.

He remembers when the Gold Star Memorial Building was the school of religion, when army barracks were used for dorms, and when Fredrickson Fieldhouse was new. Even so, Alvin said, "One thing that hasn't changed is the friendliness at OCU, and that's definitely what I love most about the university." [3] He also said he thinks that over the years the campus has changed, "For the better." [4] While Alvin has been at the university he has had many people show their appreciation. The Student Senate dedicated a sapling pear tree in his name and gave him a plaque of appreciation for his 60th birthday. Alvin has touched the lives of many faculty, staff, and students, and his kindness will always linger at Oklahoma City University.

[1] Pitsiri, Lisa, "Alvin: An OCU Legend," Focus, fall 1993, 4-5.
[2] Ibid.
[3] Pitsiri, Lisa, "Alvin: an OCU Legend," *Focus*, fall 1993, 4-5.
[4] Alvin Naifeh, personal interview, 5 Feb. 2004.

Above: Oklahoma City University was the home of the ASTEC program during the 1990s. This ASTEC worker helps youngsters better understand space.

Jennings

Dr. Stephen G. Jennings was selected by the trustees to serve as the new president He assumed the presidency on July 13, 1998,[38] and was sworn into office on April 8, 1999. The first president to receive the predentials mace, during the inaugural ceremony, Jennings announced the formation of the Commission on the Future of Oklahoma City University and issued challenges to its different schools, the athletics department, and student services. He had many goals he hoped the university would meet by the end of its centennial year, 2004, including an increase in the average ACT scores of enrolling students, more regional and national media attention, and higher rankings in national publications such as *U.S. News & World Report*.[39]

In 1999 the university announced Stars as the new athletic name and logo to begin the following fall. The OCU Chiefs women's basketball team became the NAIA National Champions after a tough season during the 1998-1999 school year.[40]

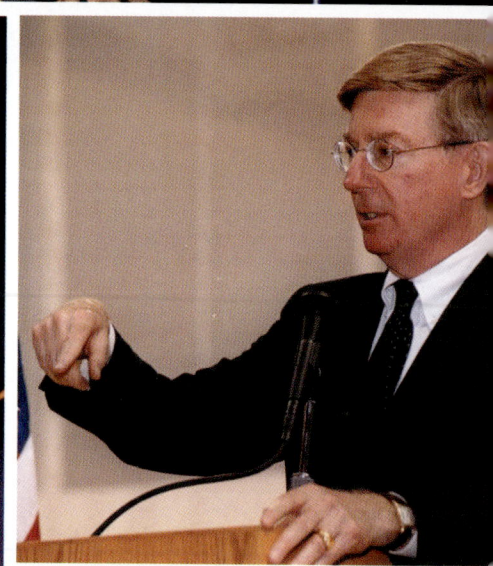

Facing a new century with faith and determination: Top row, from left: Dean Mark Parker and Wanda Bass, a trustee, donor, and namesake of the music school; Steinway pianos delivered. Middle row, from left: Students build a shack for "Shack-A-Thon," a Habitat for Humanity fund-raiser; Students volunteer at the Salvation Army. Bottom row, from left: Dance performances are a popular form of entertainment; George Will was one distinguished speaker who visited campus. Bottom right: Ann Lacy donated twelve million dollars including funds to allow the university to create a visitors center on campus.

A NEW

Chapter Ten

Century

2000

The turn of a century brought a season of change to Oklahoma City University that would see significant growth and strengthening of the student body through a renewed focus on student leadership and a campus-wide commitment to service. Political turmoil around the world brought students together for street-side protests and political debates.

New buildings were constructed and strong programs continued to grow. Many individuals invested their lives and their fortunes in "Oklahoma City's University," spending their time on the board of trustees, attending university events, supporting campus programs, and promoting private, Methodist education in Oklahoma.

President Tom J. McDaniel encouraged donors, trustees, and friends of the university to become more involved in the life and community of the university by introducing noteworthy students at events and formal meetings of the board of trustees. McDaniel also led by example in attending varsity sporting events, dance, opera, and theater productions, and student-led activities.

Students became increasingly involved in the university, sitting on committees such as the university Strategic Planning Committee and the General Education Committee. Student Senate controlled more money than ever before and governed organizations and student events held throughout the year.

Oklahoma City University spent its centennial year in service to the surrounding community, in celebration of its past achievements, and in preparation for a future as bright as its history.

The Henry J. Freede Wellness and Activity Center offered facilites for students, faculty, administrators, staff, and alumni to exercise. The center also housed the Abe Lemons Arena, named for the alumnus and beloved basketball coach, where varsity basketball games were played.

In the spring of 2000, the well-known Mid-Year Institute was replaced by the Distinguished Speaker Series lecture. The first lecture was given by Morris Dees, of the Southern Poverty Law Center, titled "Threats to America from the Radical Militia."[1] The students also had the opportunity to be part of Student Ambassadors, a small group of student volunteers dedicated to giving back to the university by giving prospective student tours and helping with dance auditions and other enrollment events.[2] Rowing was added to the campus as a club sport, allowing dedicated students to compete in the intense and rewarding activity.[3]

The Henry J. Freede Wellness and Activity Center was dedicated on March 27, 2000. It soon became the new home for Stars' athletics programs as well as a running track, training room, fitness center, and other athletic facilities.[4] The wellness center was also home to the Leichter Reunion Room, where the university held meetings and hosted many distinguished visitors.

The School of Law also honored one of its own who became the third university alumni to be appointed to the Oklahoma Supreme Court. Alumnus James R. Winchester joined alumni Marian P. Opala and Yvonne Kauger.[5] Three years later, the law school became a member of the American Association of Law Schools, a distinguished accreditation.

Tom J. McDaniel became the sixteenth president of Oklahoma City University on July 1, 2001. Originally from Alva, Oklahoma, President McDaniel had a successful career as an attorney, the chief executive officer of Kerr-McGee Corporation, and president of Northwestern Oklahoma State University, Weatherford, Oklahoma before becoming president of Oklahoma City University. President McDaniel made his mission clear when he began work at the university.[6]

> "…Oklahoma City University should aspire to
> set the standard by which private, church-related
> universities are measured. We will achieve this
> by putting student success and welfare first,
> providing a quality education that encourages
> spiritual nurturing and service, involving ourselves
> in the economic development and health of our
> neighborhood and community in a global context,
> and being the leader in cultural activity for our city
> and this state."[7]

On the evening of Sunday, December 2, 2001, the university held its first Light the Campus celebration, planned to be an annual outreach to the community surrounding Oklahoma City University and a Christmas event for faculty, administration, staff, students, and friends. The evening was highlighted by music, hot coffee and apple cider, horse-drawn carriage rides, caroling, dancing, and pictures with Santa. At the event, the Student Senate sponsored a dinner and gifts for underprivileged children in the community. This event has grown over the years, attracting many visitors to campus and giving the campus community a chance to celebrate Christmas together.[8]

The Coaching Legend
Abe Lemons at Oklahoma City University

"Simply describing Abe Lemons as a man of tremendous humor is like saying New York City is big and leaving it at that. There is a depth to Abe that very few people I have met even approach having," said Coach Bob Knight of the University of Indiana.[1]

Abe Lemons began his time at Oklahoma City University as a student in 1947. He was a standout player for the Chiefs until he graduated in 1950. At that time, basketball coach Doyle Parrack asked Lemons to become assistant basketball coach. In 1955, when Parrack took a coaching job at the University of Oklahoma, Lemons was promoted to head coach. Lemons had the distinction of being one of the first assistant coaches at any NCAA school to be promoted to head coach and was one of the youngest head coaches in the country.[2]

Lemons remained at Oklahoma City University as head coach from 1955 to 1973. During this time, the Chiefs men's basketball team was extremely successful, producing several All-American players and participating in the NCAA play-offs five times. In 1974, Lemons left Oklahoma City University to coach for Pan American, Edinburgh, Texas.[3] In 1978, Lemons was named National Coach of the Year.[4] Lemons coached for three seasons at Pan American before moving to the University of Texas in 1979.[5]

By 1983, though, Lemons was back at Oklahoma City University as head men's basketball coach. In 1985, Oklahoma City University went from NCAA to NAIA status due to the small size of the university's athletics program. The Chiefs men's basketball once again began to flourish under Lemons' leadership, and the 1986-1987 season brought a 34-1 record and a chance to compete in the NAIA national tournament for the first time. Although the Chiefs lost in the second round of the tournament, Lemons had established his team as a powerhouse in the division and a worthy contender.[6]

Lemons was remembered fondly by those who played for him and competed against him. Lemons was described as a constant teacher, willing to share stories and experiences with anyone

and invested in the lives of everyone around him.[7] "He taught us that, in life, opportunity comes to those with skill *and* tenacity," said Richard Travis, '69 Bachelor of Arts (NCAA All-American his junior and senior years).[8]

Although Lemons expected his players to work hard on the court and in the classroom, he thought it unnecessary to implement any rules that didn't directly affect the players' ability to play. "If you have a bunch of rules, sure enough somebody is going to break them. And it's probably going to be your good players,"

Lemons said. "If going to bed at 10 p.m. is going to make you play better, why not go to bed at three in the afternoon?"[9] Lemons was known to ask student workers how school was going and remind them to work toward their futures.

"Abe kept files on all of us players, and used to tell us he spent a minimum of fifteen minutes a day thinking about each specific player, and I believe it. If you had problems, he'd say, 'You'd better straighten out. I had to spend a whole hour thinking about you today.' That personal attention paid off," said Eddie Jackson, '65 Bachelor of Arts and the first black athlete to come to Oklahoma City University.[10]

In 1990, Lemons officially retired from coaching at Oklahoma City University.[11] Later that year, he was inducted into the Oklahoma Sports Hall of Fame.[12] In honor of Lemons's dedication to the university and to basketball, the sports arena of the Henry J. Freede Wellness and Activity Center was officially named the Abe Lemons Arena when the center was dedicated in 2000.

[1] "When most people think of Abe Lemons," *Focus*, summer 1999, 9.
[2] "Abe Lemons Retires June 30," *Focus*, spring 1990, 25.
[3] Ibid.
[4] *Focus*, fall 2002, 17.
[5] "Abe Lemons Retires June 30," *Focus*, spring 1990, 25.
[6] Ibid.
[7] "Abe—Back home again," *OCU Focus*, summer 1983, 27.
[8] *Focus*, fall 2002, 17.
[9] "When most people think of Abe Lemons," *Focus*, summer 1999, 9.
[10] *Focus*, fall 2002, 17.
[11] "Abe Lemons Retires June 30," *Focus*, spring 1990, 25.
[12] *Focus*, fall 2002, 17.

President Tom. J. McDaniel, Herman Meinders, LaDonna Meinders, Bill Shdeed, and Dean Bart Ward participate in the groundbreaking ceremony for the Meinders School of Business.

In November, 2001, Dr. Ann Lacy gave an unrestricted gift to the university to further private education for young people in Oklahoma.[9] Lacy's gift eventually allowed the renovation of the old United Methodist Conference Office, transforming the space into the Ann Lacy Visitor Center, a welcome center for prospective students and guests. Other generous gifts followed. Three groundbreaking ceremonies were held for new building projects in 2002. These included an expansion of the Norick Art Center, a new Meinders School of Business, and a new Wanda L. Bass School of Music as an expansion of the existing Kirkpatrick Fine Arts building. As President McDaniel worked hard to put students first, many business leaders and alumni invested in the future of the university. On July 23, 2002, the university had a groundbreaking ceremony for an expansion of the Norick Art Center. Expanded degree programs in the arts, including a new program in photography, made this expansion necessary.[10] On August 20, another groundbreaking ceremony was held for the new Meinders School of Business building project funded by former students Herman and LaDonna Meinders.[11] A gala celebration with music and many notable alumni began the groundbreaking ceremony for yet another new building on September 28, 2002. The ceremony for the Wanda L. Bass School of Music was held 75 years from the day Charles Lindbergh presided over the groundbreaking ceremony for the original School of Music building in 1927. The new school would house the gift of 105 Steinway pianos given by Dr. Bass.[12]

In spring, 2002, pilot courses were offered as part of a new program called OCU*Serves*, an initiative to introduce a community service component into courses at the university. One course, Latin American Civilization, offered students the opportunity to spend time volunteering in a bilingual classroom at Wheeler Elementary or at the Latino Community Development Center. Each semester, the commitment to service-learning grew as more courses added a community service component to coursework. Service-learning courses gave students the opportunity to work in the community and use their classroom knowledge to help others.[13]

On February 28, 2003, Tom J. McDaniel was officially inaugurated as Oklahoma City University's sixteenth president.[14] By the time of the inauguration, McDaniel had already implemented many new programs and gained the respect of faculty and students alike. During his inauguration, McDaniel promised to make the university a more student-centered campus with an even greater focus on service to the surrounding community. "People are realizing that an important part of learning is not just to make a living," McDaniel said. "It's about learning to live a life. Part of living a life is being in service to others."[15] As a part of McDaniel's service to the university, a course in leadership was offered in the spring of 2004. The course, which McDaniel co-taught with Vice President of Student Affairs Dr. Richard Hall, offered a small group of students the opportunity to interact with community leaders throughout the semester. This type of commitment was indicative of McDaniel's commitment to student success.

In spring, 2003, students on campus held the First Annual Hunger Banquet. The banquet was an event planned to make students aware of poverty in developing regions and to raise money for World Neighbors, the organization begun by Dr. John Peters as World Assistance, Inc. in the 1950s.[16] As Peters intended when he took a leave of absence from teaching at the university to begin the program, World Neighbors continued to help people in underprivileged areas into the next century.

The Lip-Sync Contest is an integral part of homecoming festivities on campus. Student organizations plan music and skits that reflect group attitudes, values, and commitment to the university and perform them before the student body.

OCU*Leads* was an organization of freshman students who were proven leaders in high school and who wished to positively impact the campus community through their time at Oklahoma City University.

During the 2003-2004 school year, many traditions from bygone years continued with homecoming festivities including a lip-sync contest, float-building, and the crowning of a homecoming king and queen. As the Oklahoma Opera and Music Theater Company celebrated its 80th season, it continued a tradition of excellence in the performing arts, and the Stars sports teams continued to compete in the NAIA, ranking among the best in the nation. Members of faculty continued to be recognized for their scholastic works as well as their commitment to the classroom. Students continued to excel in the classroom and in their careers because of dedicated faculty and staff who passionately inspire student leaders. As a part of President McDaniel's initiative to increase student involvement on campus, students sat on nearly all university committees and were active at the highest level of university governance. Matt Harney became Oklahoma City University's first student senate president to sit on the board of trustees at McDaniel's request during the fall of 2003.

Throughout Oklahoma City University's hundred-year history, many traditions have come and gone and students have changed over time. The typical OCU student is no longer the boy in knickers and a button-down shirt, gazing at a lone building on the prairie on a treeless campus. Oklahoma City University boasts a population of nearly 4,000 students from across the globe to its own back yard.

The University offers degrees in nursing, business, arts, sciences, and law. The campus focused on serving the surrounding community through tutoring programs, internships, and development of skills through service-based learning. Students became involved in all levels of campus leadership both on campus and in the community.

Although organizations were primarily closed in the early years of the university, in 2004 most student organizations were open organizations, requiring no bid process for entrance. Over time organizations became less about academics and became more focused on the social needs of the students. Organizations like OCU*Leads*, the Black Student Association, Student Senate, and the National Women's Law Student Association addressed a diverse student population. Students participated in varsity sports such as basketball, baseball, softball, soccer, golf, and crew, while continuing to be active in policy and government by promoting political and social change both on

148

A university professor leads a writing group at Epworth Villa, a Methodist Retirement Community. Students and faculty donated their time to work in the community in bilingual elementary classrooms, community centers, and retirement centers, learning through helping others.

Diversity in education: Top: President Tom J. McDaniel greets students as they cross the stage at the graduation ceremony. Bottom from left: Dance performances on campus are well attended by the university community; students learn through hands-on work and seminar-type discussions.

and off campus.

Faith continued to hold a special place on campus, with chapel services being the only item scheduled every Thursday at 1:00 p.m. Faith-based organizations also played a vital role in the campus community, nurturing students both mentally and spiritually.

While many substantial gifts were made to the university in the last four years of Oklahoma City University's century of service, the importance of students and faculty and their service to the community and the world made the greatest impact on the campus and community in the last hundred years. Oklahoma City University has spent a century in service to the city, the state, the church, and the nation, addressing both local and global needs with the help of individuals invested in the success of students and in the future of the university.

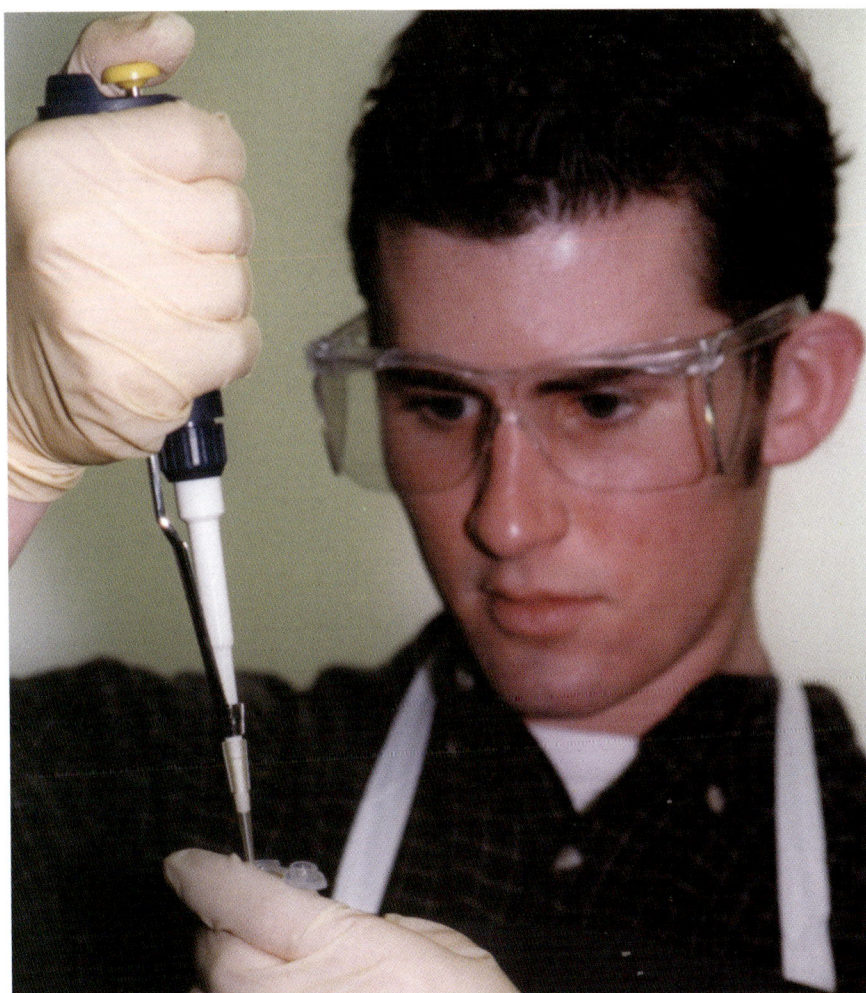

Oklahoma City University

Information Contributed By: Scott P. Kedy

R.B. McSwain

R. B. McSwain was named president of Epworth University in 1904. He had been registrar of Southwestern University at Georgetown, Texas. McSwain was studying for his doctorate at the University of Chicago when he was appointed to the presidency. He had received a bachelor of arts degree from Arkadelphia Methodist College in his home state of Arkansas and a masters degree from Vanderbilt University in Tennessee. After only a few months of service to the budding institution, McSwain suffered a series of health problems and resigned.

G. C. Jones

Dr. G. C. Jones succeeded President McSwain as the second president of Epworth University. Jones, a professor of chemistry, was elected to complete the first scholastic year at the new university after McSwain's health began to deteriorate.

George Bradford

At the age of 34, George Henry Bradford accepted the role of university chancellor. Born in Morrisville, Indiana, Bradford held degrees from Missouri Wesleyan University, Sacred Theology, and the University of Denver. He held an honorary doctorate from Carrolton College. After the closing of Epworth University, Bradford remained in office for one year, serving as president of Oklahoma Methodist College until 1912.

William Fielder

President William Fielder became the second president of Oklahoma Methodist University in 1912, serving the institution for the early and most turbulent years. Fielder had worked as the university's vice chancellor and had "proven his qualifications for the work...by his application, energy and effectiveness." During Fielder's tenure the institution was described as "a denominational school... not sectarian ... [but] an environment conducive to cultivation of clean, sane Christian character."

Edward Hislop

Edward Hislop fulfilled the role of president from 1914 to 1918. Born in Steubenville, Ohio, in May, 1873, Hislop spent most of his childhood in Kansas, raised by a Scotsman father and a mother from Virginia. He graduated from Baker University in 1903, and four years later received another degree from Boston University. Hislop believed that both the church and the university should be leaders in the community.

Edwin G. Green

Edwin George Green was president of Oklahoma Methodist University from 1918 to 1919, and, upon the university's closure in 1919, followed most of the faculty to its new home at Oklahoma City College. Green was born the son of a minister in Yorkshire, New York, on March 24, 1884. He received his bachelor of arts degree from the University of Denver, in Denver, Colorado, in 1906, and worked until 1910 as a high school principal in Colorado, when he moved to Fort Worth University, Fort Worth, Texas. Green would remain president of Oklahoma City College until 1923.

Eugene Antrim

Eugene M. Antrim had the experience of leading the university during a time of economic boom. During his term as president, 1923 to 1934, the institution changed its name from "college" to "university," began to grow, and became an accredited university.

Walter S. Athearn

After President Antrim's death, Walter S. Athearn served as president for the remainder of the year. Athearn, born in Iowa, received his teaching certificate from the Iowa Normal College in 1892. Eight years later he received a Bachelor of Pedagogy degree from Drake University and then served as the dean of Highland Park Normal College. He returned to Drake in 1909 as a professor while continuing his studies. He earned a bachelor of arts degree in 1911 and a master of arts degree in 1914 from Iowa State University.

153

A.G. Williamson

C. Q. Smith

Jack Wilkes

John Olson

A. G. Williamson, president of the board of trustees and pastor of Wesley Methodist Church, became the university president in December 1934. Williamson, a 1916 graduate of Oklahoma Methodist University, was the first alumnus to serve as president. Williamson accepted the office fully aware of the institution's financial struggles. During his seven-year tenure, Williamson strove to decrease the amount of debt.

Dr. Cluster Quentin Smith was born in Stephenville, Texas, on March 27, 1890. He became president on June 1, 1941. Smith had the unique challenge of leading the university while the nation was at war. Smith held the reins of the university for 16 years. Under his guidance, Oklahoma City University grew faster than ever before. He inherited many problems, but always found ways to overcome them. The student-faculty center was later named for C.Q. Smith.

Dr. Jack Stauffer Wilkes held the office of president from 1957 to 1963. Wilkes established a partnership with M.I.T. to forge the Great Plan. Wilkes had been the pastor of Crown Heights Methodist Church in Oklahoma City. Born in Honey Grove, Texas, and a graduate of Hendrix College, he later earned a bachelor's degree from Southern Methodist University. He continued his graduate work at the University of Denver, Northwestern University, and Union Theological Seminary in Virginia. Wilkes also held an honorary doctorate from McMurray College.

Dr. John Fredrick Olson became president of the university on June 1, 1964. Born in 1919, Olson was the son of a Methodist minister. He received his A.B. from DePauw University in 1941 and was later a *summa cum laude* graduate of Boston University. He received his Ph.D. in history of theology in 1949. Upon moving to Oklahoma City University the Olsons were excited about the prospects of working with M.I.T. as well as the university's students.

Dolphus Whitten

In January 1970, Dolphus Whitten, who on several occasions had served as the university's acting president, was appointed president. Whitten was deeply committed to the church and to service to the community. Whitten was an Arkansas native, earning his bachelor of arts from Ouachita College in 1936. He received both his master of arts and Ph.D. from the University of Texas. Whitten had also served as a member of faculty at Henderson College in Arkadelphia, Arkansas, prior to his tenure at Oklahoma City University.

Jerald Walker

Dr. Jerald C. Walker took to the presidency in 1979. Under Walker's direction, the budget increased from $3.6 million in 1978 to nearly $10 million when he resigned. Walker also was instrumental in forming many of the study abroad programs that are still offered at Oklahoma City University today. His tenure also saw the founding of KOCU-TV and establishment of many degree programs, including liberal arts, computer science, and entertainment business.

Stephen Jennings

The next president, Stephen Jennings was known for setting goals for each of the schools to meet by the centennial. As president, he attempted to raise the entrance standards and increase the graduation rates. He was concerned with involving the university in the community.

Tom J. McDaniel

Tom J. McDaniel became president in July of 2001. His tenure has seen many landmark events, including dedications of an expansion to the Norick Art Center, the Ann Lacy Admissions and Visitor Center, and the Meinders School of Business. McDaniel was influential in renewing community involvement in Oklahoma City University.

Final Reference

Chapter One : Rough Beginnings

1 Clustor Q. Smith, *Building for Tomorrow* (Nashville, Tennessee: Parthenon Press, 1961), 20.

2 H.E. Brill, *The Story of Oklahoma City University* (Nashville, Tennessee: Parthenon Press, 1961), 9.

3 *Focus*, spring 1962, 20.

4 Brill, *The Story of Oklahoma City University*, 20-21.

5 Ibid., 27.

6 *The Wind-Up.* (Epworth University, 1908), 9.

7 Paul W. Milhouse, *Oklahoma City University: A Miracle at Twenty-Third and Blackwelder* (Muskogee, OK. Oklahoma Heritage Association, 1984).

8 Brill, *The Story of Oklahoma City University*, 28.

9 Brill, *The Story of Oklahoma City University*, 32.

10 Smith, *Building for Tomorrow*, 24.

11 Ibid., 25-26.

12 Ibid., 27-28.

13 Brill, *The Story of Oklahoma City University*, 32.

14 Smith, *Building for Tomorrow*, 27-28.

15 Ibid., 34.

16 Brill, *The Story of Oklahoma City University*, 33.

17 George L. Harrell, "Epworth University: Yesterday, Today, and Tomorrow," *The Campus*, Nov. 1907, 3-6.

18 Harwell, "Epworth University: Yesterday, Today, and Tomorrow," 4.

19 Smith, *Building for Tomorrow*, 34.

20 Ibid., 35.

21 Brill, *The Story of Oklahoma City University*, 46-52.

22 *Report of the Board of Trustees Concerning Epworth University*, 3 January 1911.

23 Smith, *Building for Tomorrow*, 36.

24 Smith, *Building for Tomorrow*, 37.

25 Brill, *The Story of Oklahoma City University*, 69.

26 Smith, *Building for Tomorrow*, 49.

27 Brill, *The Story of Oklahoma City University*, 77-78.

28 Smith, *Building for Tomorrow*, 52-53.

29 Brill, *The Story of Oklahoma City University*, 94-95.

Chapter Two: The Golden Age

1 Smith, *Building for Tomorrow*, 62.

2 Brill, *The Story of Oklahoma City University*, 106.

3 Ibid.,114-115.

4 Oklahoma City College, *The Rambler* (Oklahoma City, Oklahoma: Class of 1921, 1921), 98.

5 "School for Training Religious Leaders Opened November 16," *The Campus*. 8 Nov. 1920, 1, 3.

6 "Launching Sunday," *The Campus*, 15 April 1921, 1, 3.

7 "Review Sunday Shows Progress in Campaign," *The Campus*, 1 May 1921, 1.

Endnotes

8 "Campaign Committee and Trustees Will Meet," *The Campus*, 1 June 1921, 1.

9 "Troutman Third in Half Mile Race," *The Campus*, 1 May 1921, 1.

10 "Enrollment Equals 250 Mark," *The Campus*, 15 Nov. 1921, 2.

11 "OCC Enters Conference," *The Campus*, 15 Dec. 1921, 1.

12 "Wrestling Team Formed," *The Campus*, 15 Dec. 1921, 2.

13 "The Golgbugs Appear," *The Campus*, Oct. 1921, 1.

14 Millhouse, *Oklahoma City University: A Miracle at Twenty-Third and Blackwelder*, 45.

15 Millhouse, *Oklahoma City University: A Miracle at Twenty-Third and Blackwelder*, 48.

16 Smith, *Building for Tomorrow*, 66.

17 Brill, *The Story of Oklahoma City University*, 111-113.

18 Oklahoma City College, *The Scarab* (1923), 59-65.

19 "Men's Dorm," *The Campus*, 10 Jan. 1922, 1.

20 "Business Administration Course to be offered," *The Campus*, 10 Jan. 1922, 1.

21 Frizzell, 2 Jan. 2003.

22 Milhouse, *Oklahoma City University: A Miracle at Twenty-Third and Blackwelder*, 52.

23 Brill, *The Story of Oklahoma City University*, 140.

24 Milhouse, *Oklahoma City University: A Miracle at Twenty-Third and Blackwelder*, 58.

25 Brill, *The Story of Oklahoma City University*, 140.

26 Smith, *Building for Tomorrow*, 73.

27 Brill, *The Story of Oklahoma City University*, 140.

28 Ibid., 143.

29 Ibid., 142.

30 Milhouse, *Oklahoma City University: A Miracle at Twenty-Third and Blackwelder*, 59.

31 Ibid.

32 Brill *The Story of Oklahoma City University*, 143.

33 Milhouse, *Oklahoma City University: A Miracle at Twenty-Third and Blackwelder*, 53.

34 Smith, *Building for Tomorrow*, 73.

35 Milhouse, *Oklahoma City University: A Miracle at Twenty-Third and Blackwelder*, 54.

36 Ibid., 60.

37 "Geraldine Patton Writes School Song," *The Campus*, 22 Sept. 1925, 1.

38 Professor C. M. Allen, "Evening College is Unique School: Department Designed for Part Time Students," *The Campus*, 5 Nov. 1925, 1, 3.

39 Milhouse, *Oklahoma City University: A Miracle at Twenty-Third and Blackwelder*, 56.

40 "Sport Mixture," *The Campus*, 16 September 1925, 4.

41 "Sports Mixture: Archery Begins," *The Campus*, 5 Oct. 1925, 4.

42 Oklahoma City University, *The Scarab*, 1926.

43 "Forty Candidates in Daily Workout: Nine Hard Tilts Ahead for Goldbug Squad this Year," *The Campus*, 16 Sept. 1925, 1.

44 Oklahoma City University, *The Scarab*, 1926.

45 "OCU Wins Place in State Relays," *The Campus*, 24 May 1926, 1, 4.

46 "Students Earn Living: Picking Campus Cotton," *The Campus*, 16 Sept. 1925, 2.

47 "Convention Gives Cotton as Favor," *The Campus*, 5 Oct. 1925, 3.

48 Smith, *Building for Tomorrow*, 75.

49 Brill, *The Story of Oklahoma City University*, 144.

50 "Frosh Caps," *The Campus*, 10 Sept. 1926, 2.

51 "Freshmen Burn Caps at Thanksgiving Game," *The Campus*, 3 Dec. 1926, 1.

52 Smith, *Building for Tomorrow*, 78.

53 "OCU Basketball Opens Season with Maverick Scrap Tonight," *The Campus*, 16 Dec. 1925, 3.

54 "New Gym Will Seat Nearly Five Hundred," *The Campus*, 11 Jan. 1926, 2.

55 Smith, *Building for Tomorrow*, 79.

56 "Temporary Gym Being Erected," *The Campus*, 22 Sept. 1925, 2.

57 "New Gym to be of Gothic Type," *The Campus*, 5 Oct. 1925, 2.

58 "42nd to 9th in Rank," *The Campus*, 8 Feb. 1926, 3.

59 "OCU to Raise 1,500,000 Dollars," *The Campus*, 15 Feb. 1926, 1.

60 "OCU Students Set Campus Campaign at $70,000," *The Campus*, 8 March 1926, 1.

61 "Unification of Two Methodisms," *The Campus*, 15 March 1926, 1, 4.

62 Ibid.

63 Smith, *Building for Tomorrow*, 75-76.

64 Milhouse, *Oklahoma City University: A Miracle at Twenty-Third and Blackwelder*, 64-

65.
[65] Smith, *Building for Tomorrow,* 80.
[66] Frizzell, Mildred. Interviewed by Ryan McGee and Rebecca Fenton, 2 Jan. 2004.
[67] Brill, *The Story of Oklahoma City University,* 148.
[68] Milhouse, *Oklahoma City University: A Miracle at Twenty-Third and Blackwelder,* 67.
[69] Franklin, Rev. S.W., ed. *Journal of the Eighteenth Session of the West Oklahoma Annual Conference of the Methodist Episcopal Church South,* 7-11 Nov. 1928.
[70] Smith, *Building for Tomorrow,* 77.

Chapter Three: The Lean Years

[1] "OCU Foreseen As One of Biggest Educational Institutions of Country," *The Torch,* Sept. 1929, 1.
[2] Oklahoma Methodist-Episcopal Church South Conference. 85th Session, (Boston Avenue Church, Tulsa, 1930), 85.
[3] Ibid., 86.
[4] Brill, *The Story of Oklahoma City University,* 151.
[5] Frizzell, 3 Jan. 2004.
[6] Smith, *Building for Tomorrow,* 86.
[7] Ibid., 84.
[8] Frizzell, 2 Jan. 2004.
[9] Milhouse, *Oklahoma City University: A Miracle at Twenty-Third and Blackwelder,* 73.
[10] Brill, *The Story of Oklahoma City University,* 177.
[11] Smith, *Building for Tomorrow,* 85.
[12] Brill, *The Story of Oklahoma City University,* 196b.
[13] Ibid., 196a.
[14] Oklahoma Annual Conference Methodist-Episcopal Church South, 86th session, (St. Luke's Church, Oklahoma City, 1931), 55.
[15] Oklahoma Annual Conference Methodist-Episcopal Church South, 87th session, (Boston Avenue Church, Tulsa, 1932), 57.
[16] Brill, *The Story of Oklahoma City University,* 171.
[17] Oklahoma Methodist-Episcopal Annual Conference, 88th session, (St. Luke's Church, Oklahoma City, 1933), 54.
[18] Oklahoma Methodist-Episcopal Church South Conference, 89th session, (First Methodist-Episcopal Church, Ardmore, 1934), 49.
[19] Milhouse, *Oklahoma City University: A Miracle at Twenty-Third and Blackwelder,* 83.
[20] Brill, *The Story of Oklahoma City University,* 156.
[21] Milhouse, *Oklahoma City University: A Miracle at Twenty-Third and Blackwelder,* 89.
[22] Smith, *Building for Tomorrow,* 92.
[23] Milhouse, *Oklahoma City University: A Miracle at Twenty-Third and Blackwelder,* 89-90.
[24] Ibid.
[25] Oklahoma Annual Conference Journal: Methodist-Episcopal Church, South, 90th session, (St. Paul's Church, Muskogee, 1935).
[26] Brill, *The Story of Oklahoma City University,* 194.
[27] Ibid., 177.
[28] Milhouse, *Oklahoma City University: A Miracle at Twenty-Third and Blackwelder,* 97.
[29] "Student Boxing Coach has Interesting Career," *The Campus,* 15 Dec. 1939, 4.
[30] "Rev. H. E. Brill Publishes Story of OCU," *The Campus,* 29 Sept. 1939, 3.
[31] Smith, *Building for Tomorrow,* 83.

Chapter Four: War and Growth

[1] Smith, *Building for Tomorrow,* 109.
[2] West Oklahoma Conference, 3rd Session, (Ardmore, 1941), 249.
[3] Smith, *Building for Tomorrow,* 108-109.
[4] Ibid., 112.
[5] Milhouse, *Oklahoma City University: A Miracle at Twenty-Third and Blackwelder,* 107.
[6] Bennett, Paul, ed. "Homecoming," *The AlumNews,* Oct. 1941, 3.
[7] Bennett, "Homecoming," 3.
[8] Milhouse, *Oklahoma City University: A Miracle at Twenty-Third and Blackwelder,* 110-111.
[9] Bennett, "Homecoming," 6.
[10] Milhouse, *Oklahoma City University: A Miracle at Twenty-Third and Blackwelder,* 111.
[11] Bennett, "Homecoming," 2.
[12] West Oklahoma Conference of the Methodist Church, 3rd-11th annual sessions: 1941-1949.
[13] Bennett, "Homecoming," 10.
[14] Smith, *Building for Tomorrow,* 124.
[15] Bennett, *The AlumNews,* vol. 3, no. 2: Jan. 1942.
[16] Bennett, Jan. 1942, 5.
[17] Oklahoma City University. "The Inauguration of Clustor Quentin Smith as President of Oklahoma City University,"

Oklahoma City, Oklahoma, 16 Jan. 1942.

[18] "Eighth President Inaugurated," *The West Oklahoma Methodist,* Jan. 1942, 1.

[19] Oklahoma City University, 1942, 1.

[20] C. Q. Smith, "Inaugural Address" (Speech given on the occasion of his inauguration as the eighth president of Oklahoma City University, Oklahoma City, Oklahoma, 16 January 1942).

[21] Smith, C. Q., "Brief Description of Oklahoma City University Prior to Arrival of Training Detachment," (University Archives, Oklahoma City, Oklahoma).

[22] "O.C.U. to Offer Defense Courses in Second Term," *The Campus,* 11 Jan. 1944, 1.

[23] Bennett, Paul, ed., *The AlumNew,* vol. 3, May 1942, 1.

[24] "New Cadet Aviation Center Opens: Students Housed at Fair Grounds in Fine Buildings: Training Detachment is Definitely a Part of O.C.U," *The Campus,* 21 May 1943, 1.

[25] Milhouse, *Oklahoma City University: A Miracle at Twenty-Third and Blackwelder,* 113-114.

[26] "OCU Purchases Flying Field," *The Campus,* 24 May 1943, 1.

[27] West Oklahoma Conference. 4th session (Oklahoma City, 14-18 Oct. 1942), 397.

[28] Milhouse, *Oklahoma City University: A Miracle at Twenty-Third and Blackwelder,* 113.

[29] West Oklahoma Conference of the Methodist Church, 5th session (Oklahoma City, Oklahoma, 12-15 October 1943), 193.

[30] "O.C.U. Service Roll Contains 477 Names," *The Campus,* 15 Sept. 1943, 4.

[31] "War Program," *The Campus,* 14 Oct. 1943, 2.

[32] "O.C.U. Receives Service Award," *The Campus,* 6 July 1944, 1.

[33] Smith, *Building for Tomorrow,* 147.

[34] "Banning Gift," *The Campus,* 14 Oct. 1943, 2

[35] Smith, *Building for Tomorrow,* 175.

[36] Ibid., 150-152.

[37] "O.C.U. Music School Receives National Honor," *The Campus,* 31 March 1944, 1.

[38] Smith, *Building for Tomorrow,* 154.

[39] "Kickoff Dinner Opens Campaign Tonight at 7: 10,000 needed volumes in Last Vital Step for accreditation," *The Campus,* 23 June 1944, 1, 4.

[40] "O.C.U. Submits 3 Pictures for Pin-Up Contest: Sororities, Independents Pick Candidates for Tito Guizar Judging," *The Campus,* 15 Dec. 1944, 1.

[41] "Guizar selects Pin-Up Winners," *The Campus,* 12 Jan. 1945, 1.

[42] "Wind and Lightning Damage OCU Tower," *The Campus,* 2 March 1945, 1.

[43] Smith, *Building for Tomorrow,* 168.

[44] Milhouse, *Oklahoma City University: A Miracle at Twenty-Third and Blackwelder,* 119.

[45] "Memorial will be Wednesday," *The Campus,* 4 May 1945, 1.

[46] "Former Student Signed by MGM Pictures Studio," *The Campus,* 7 Dec. 1945, 4; "Ann Steely, Former Student, Will Soon Appear in First Movie," *The Campus,* 6 Dec. 1946, 4.

[47] "Enrollment Closes with Total of 2040," *The Campus,* 8 Feb. 1946, 1.

[48] Smith, *Building for Tomorrow,* 170.

[49] "Land Lease Offer Accepted by Navy: Executive Committee Agrees to Armory Site on Campus," *The Campus,* 27 Sept. 1946, 1.

[50] "New Buildings Soon to be Moved to OCU Campus," *The Campus,* 15 Nov. 1946, 1; "Housing Project Continues," *The Campus,* 4 Oct. 1946, 3.

[51] "What is IBM? Here are Facts on New System," *The Campus,* 27 Sept. 1946, 3.

[52] "'Chiefs are Born as 'Thunderbirds,' 'Goldbugs' Retire," *The Campus,* 13 Sept. 1946, 7.

[53] "Tennis Stars Attend O.C.U.," *The Campus,* 22 Feb. 1946, 4; "Tennis Stars Defeat El Reno Twosome," *The Campus,* April 1946, 4; "Net Men Defeat Norman Teams," *The Campus,* 17 April 1946, 4; "Stewart is a Scholar, Athlete, Poet," *The Campus,* 14 November 1947, 4.

[54] Smith, *Building for Tomorrow,* 172-173.

[55] "OCU Gold Star Memorial," *The Campus,* 10 Oct. 1947, 1.

[56] *The Campus,* 14 Oct. 1949, 1.

[57] *The Campus,* 16 Sept. 1949, 1.

[58] Ibid.

[59] *The Campus,* 23 Sept. 1949, 4.

[60] Milhouse, Paul W. *Oklahoma City University* (Muskogee, OK: 1984), 127.

[61] *The Campus,* 14 Oct. 1949, 4.

Chapter Five: Our Community

[1] *Oklahoma City University Bulletin,* Oct. 1950.

[2] Ibid., Nov. 1950.

[3] Ibid., Dec. 1950.

[24] 1954 *Keshena* Yearbook, pg. 4
[25] Ibid., pg. 5
[26] 1957 *Keshena* Yearbook, pg. 26
[27] Ibid., 48; Milhouse, Paul W., *Oklahoma City University*. (Muskogee, OK: 1984), 137.
[28] *Oklahoma City University Bulletin*, June 1954.
[29] Ibid., Oct. 1954.
[30] Ibid., Dec. 1954.
[31] Ibid.
[32] *Oklahoma City University Bulletin*, April 1955.
[33] 1955 *Keshena* Yearbook, 23.
[34] *Oklahoma City University Bulletin*, May 1955.
[35] Ibid., June 1955, 4.
[36] Ibid., April 1955.
[37] Ibid., April 1955.
[38] Ibid., May 1955, 4.
[39] Ibid., June 1955, 1.
[40] Ibid., June 1955, 1.
[41] Ibid.
[42] Ibid.; "They're off and singing…,"*Focus*, summer, 10-11.
[43] *Oklahoma City University Bulletin*, September 1955, 1, 4.
[44] *Oklahoma City University Bulletin*, July 1955, 1.
[45] Ibid.
[46] *Oklahoma City University Bulletin*, Oct. 1955, 1.
[47] Ibid., 3
[48] Ibid.
[49] *Oklahoma City University Bulletin*, Aug. 1956, 1.
[50] Ibid., 4.
[51] 1957 *Keshena*, 193.
[52] 1957 *Keshena*, 192.
[53] *Alumni News OCU*, spring 1957, 3.
[54] Ibid., 4.
[55] 1958 *Keshena*, 18.
[56] *Alumni News OCU*, summer 1957, 3.
[57] Ibid., fall 1957, 3.
[58] Ibid., 8.
[59] *Keshena*, 21.
[60] *Alumni News OCU*, spring 1958, 3-6.
[61] *Alumni News OCU*, spring 1958, 11.
[62] Ibid., summer 1958, 3.
[63] Ibid., 7.
[64] Ibid., 12.
[65] Ibid., fall 1958, 6.

[4] Ibid., Feb. 1951.
[5] *Oklahoma City University Bulletin*, May 1951.
[6] Ibid., July 1951.
[7] Ibid., Aug. 1951.
[8] Milhouse, Paul W., *Oklahoma City University* (Muskogee, OK: 1984), 130.
[9] *Oklahoma City University Bulletin*, Dec. 1951.
[10] Ibid., Dec. 1951 and May 1952.
[11] Ibid., Jan. 1952.
[12] *Oklahoma City University Bulletin*, Feb. 1952.
[13] Ibid.
[14] Ibid., March 1952.
[15] Milhouse, Paul W., *Oklahoma City University*, (Muskogee, Oklahoma: 1984), 133.
[16] *Oklahoma City University Bulletin*, May 1952.
[17] *Focus*, fall 1965, 6-7.
[18] *Alumni News OCU*, winter 1960, 5.
[19] *The Campus*, Sept. 18, 1952, 2.
[20] Ibid., 4.
[21] Ibid., Oct. 2, 1952. 4.
[22] Ibid.
[23] Ibid., Oct. 9, 1952, 1.

66 Ibid., spring 1959, 3.
67 Alumni News OCU, spring 1959, 4
68 Ibid., 8.
69 Ibid., fall 1959, 2.

Chapter Six: New Partnership

1 *Alumni News OCU*, winter 1960, 2
2 Ibid., 3.
3 Ibid., 4
4 *Focus*, winter 1966, 2-3
5 *Alumni News OCU*, summer 1960, 5.
6 *Focus*, fall 1960, 4.
7 Ibid., 10.
8 Ibid., 4.
9 Ibid., 8.
10 *Focus*, winter 1963, 23.
11 Ibid., 4.
12 Ibid., 4.
13 Ibid., 3.
14 *Focus*, spring 1964, 2.
15 Ibid., 3.
16 Ibid., cover.
17 Ibid., 4-5.
18 Focus, fall 1964, 1.
19 Ibid., 8-9.
20 Ibid., winter 1964-1965, 2-3.
21 Ibid., winter 1964-1965, 4-5
22 *Focus*, winter 1964-1965, 12-13
23 Ibid., 18.
24 Ibid., summer 1965, 1.
25 Ibid., fall 1966, 3.
26 Ibid., fall 1967, 3-4.
27 *Focus*, fall 1967, 1-2, and 18.
28 Ibid., spring 1968, 3 and 5.
29 *Focus*, spring 1968, 10.
30 *Focus*, spring 1968, 8-9.
31 Ibid., 11-26.
32 Ibid., winter 1968-1969, 2.
33 Ibid., 3.
34 Ibid., Sept. 18, 1969, 2.
35 Ibid., Sept. 11, 1969.
36 Ibid., Sept. 24, 1969, 2-3.
37 Ibid., Oct. 2, 1969, 3.
38 *The Campus*, October 17, 1969, pg. 1
39 *The Campus*, November 14, 1969, pg. 2

Chapte Seven: Out of the Box

1 *The Campus*, 23 Jan. 1970, 1.
2 Idid., 6 Mar. 1970, 1.
3 Ibid., 10 Apr. 1970, 4.
4 "Whitten Inaugurated Ninth President,"
bi-focus, Feb. 1971, 1.
5 "Present Crisis—Future Hope," *bi-focus*, Feb. 1971, 3.
6 "Business…Aviation….," *bi-focus*, Feb. 1971, 5.
7 "Razzle Dazzle Dancin,'" *Focus*. Spring 1985, 18-19.
8 "The OCU Chiefs: sight on the playoffs," *Focus*. winter 1981, 14-15.
9 *Alumni Focus OCU*, Sept. 1975, 8-9.
10 *Alumni Focus OCU*, Sept. 1975, 3.
11 "Experience Counts with OCU's Alternative Degree Program," *OCU Focus*, summer 1985, 7.
12 *Alumni Focus OCU*, Dec. 1977, 12.
13 *Alumni Focus OCU*, Mar. 1977, 13
14 "Cymbals Clash, Drums Roll for Summer Band," *Alumni Focus*, July 1978, 3-4.
15 "A Message from the University's President," *Alumni Focus*, July 1978, 9.
16 "Mid-Year Institute Explores Role of Big Government," *Alumni Focus*, Jan. 1979, 6.
17 "Mid-Year Institute Explores Role of Big Government," *Alumni Focus*, Jan. 1979, 7.
18 "Dr. Whitten: Past and Future," *Alumni Focus*, Jan. 1979, 10.
19 "President Whitten Reflects on His Life at OCU," *Alumni Focus*, Jan. 1979, 3-5.
20 "Good Memories and Strong Hopes," *Focus*. fall 1979, 3-4.
21 "The New Law School Facilities: It's something to be proud of, students say," *Focus*. Winter 1980, 9-10.
22 "Dr. and Mrs. Whitten Retire Move To North Carolina," *Focus*. fall 1979, 16.
23 1980. A Celebration. *Focus*. winter. 4-7.

Chapter Eight: Go International

1 "Fourth Annual Pow-Wow Held," *Focus*, spring 1984, 9.
2 "School of Law Dedication April 23," *Focus*, spring 1981, 3.
3 Ibid., 3.
4 "Computer Science added at OCU," *Focus*. spring 1981. 6.
5 "Dance Program Launched," *Focus*. spring 1981. 7.
6 Jerald Walker, "Our House is in Order," *Focus*. summer 1981. 2.
7 Ibid.
8 "Bob Hope, Susan Powell and Friends Thrill OCU Audience," Ibid., 4-5.
9 "Virginia Walker Brings the Stars—and

Money—to OCU," *Focus*. Fall 1984, 22-23.
[10] "Fencers Finish with Impressive Record," *Focus,* summer 1984, 23.
[11] "A Decade of Progress." *Focus,* spring 1989, 6.
[12] " OCU's Miss America receives royal welcome," *Focus,* winter 1981, 4-5.
[13] " A Decade of Progress," *Focus,* spring 1989, 6.
[14] "OCU's First Ever Mascot Unveiled at Homecoming," *Focus,* winter 1981, 14-15.
[15] " Roy Clark," *Focus,* summer 1982, 4-5.
[16] " Foundation Curriculum," *Focus,* summer 1982, 11.
[17] " OCU Develops Degree: OCU Comes to the Rescue as Music Becomes Big Business," *Focus,* summer 1982, 19.
[18] "The Oklahoma Opera and Musical Theatre Company," *OCU Focus,* fall 1982, 16.
[19] "Paintin' The Town: OCU's Art Department Takes on a Mega-Project as They Tackle Warehouse District Megamurals," *Ibid.,* 17.
[20] *OCU Focus,* fall 1982, 19.
[21] "English Writing Center Created," *OCU Focus,* fall 1982, 22.
[22] "New Facilities, New Players Highlight Baseball," *OCU Focus,* fall 1982, 26-27.
[23] "Lady Chiefs Slate Tour of 'Hot Spots,'" *OCU Focus,* fall 1982, 28.
[24] "Dr. Rigual Sponsors Building Renovations," *Focus,* spring 1983, 3.
[25] "Nursing Takes Realistic View of Holistic Health," *Focus,* spring 1983, 5.
[26] "OCU/Phillips Institute New Law/Theology Dual Degree," *OCU Focus,* summer 1983, 15.
[27] "OCU/SMU to Offer Doctorate," *OCU Focus,* summer 1983, 16.
[28] 1983.
[29] "The Weekend College—OCU's Alternative to Traditional Scheduling," *OCU Focus,* fall 1983, 13.
[30] "Noble Center Open for Business," *Ibid.,* 14.
[31] "Abe Reigns Once Again," *OCU Focus,* fall 1983, 17.
[32] "OCU Captures Top Golf Prize," *Focus,* summer 1984, 22.
[33] "A Decade of Progress," *Focus,* spring 1989, 7.
[34] Ibid.
[35] "West Meets East," *Focus,* spring 1984, 12-13.
[36] "A Decade of Progress," *Focus,* spring 1989, 8.
[37] "OCU Makes News With M.B.A. in China," *OCU Focus,* summer 1985, 7.
[38] "Softball Team Plays Top Teams, Wins Tourney, Sets New Records," *OCU Focus,* summer 1985, 22.
[39] "A Decade of Progress," *Focus,* spring 1989, 8.
[40] *OCU Focus,* summer 1985, 4-5.
[41] "Church and Campus—Partners in Mission," *OCU Focus,* summer 1985, 23.
[42] "Research Center Solves Business Problems, Receives SBI Designation," *Focus,* fall 1986, 10.
[43] "MBA in China Result of Long Discussions, Hard Work," *Focus,* fall 1986, 12.
[44] "OCU Teams Sweep Through NAIA Rankings," *Focus,* fall 1986, 27.
[45] "A Decade of Progress," *Focus,* spring 1989, 8.
[46] "School of Music Named for Margaret E. Petree," *Focus,* fall 1986, 16.
[47] "What's Black and White and Kicked All Over Town? OCU Soccer!" *Focus,* fall 1986, 26.
[48] "Troubled Banking Industry Topic of MLA Class," *Focus,* 1987, 14.
[49] "Dance program soars under stellar leadership," *Focus,* summer 1987.
[50] "Chiefs Finish Record-Breaking Season with Single Heartbreaking Defeat in the NAIA Nationals," *Focus,* spring 1987, 28.
[51] "OCU Renews Program with Police Administration of Republic of China," *Focus,* fall 1992, 7.
[52] "School of Religion Named in Honor of Wimberlys," *Focus,* spring 1989, 16.
[53] "A Decade of Progress," *Focus,* spring 1989, 9.
[54] "Agreements with AT&T, Multimedia Cablevision Make OCU 'Campus of Tomorrow.'" *Focus,* spring 1989, 11.
[55] "A Decade of Progress," *Focus,* spring 1989, 10.
[56] "Development Momentum in the 1990s," *Focus,* spring 1989, 13.
[57] "Teeter Handcrafts Wooden Mace for OCU President's Office," *Focus,* spring 1989, 19.
[58] "Construction Underway on New Petree College Building," *Focus,* winter 1989, 1.
[59] 1989. OCU Makes History with Soviet

Management Program. *Focus.* Winter. 7.

Chapter Nine: Home at the Top

[1] "Larry Webb Directs the new OCU Television Station," *Focus,* spring 1990, 11.
[2] "KOCU-TV Hits the Airwaves," *Focus.* Fall 1990, 47.
[3] "New Arts and Sciences Building Opens on Schedule," *Focus.* Fall 1990, 46-47.
[4] "OCU Leader in Writing Center Services for Students," *Focus.* Fall 1990, 46-47.
[5] "OCU Named Mentor for Argentina's First Methodist University," *Focus.* Spring 1990, 30.
[6] "OCU to Provide Management Education in Czech and Slovak Federal Republic," *Focus.* Spring 1991, 30.
[7] "The Chiefs Do It Again," *Focus.* Spring 1992, 4-5.
[8] "Chris Merritt to do Benefit Concert," *Focus.* Fall 1991, 48.
[9] "Campus Television Station Gets Bigger and Better," *Focus.* Spring 1991, 10-11.
[10] "The Chiefs Do It Again," *Focus.* Spring 1992, 4-5.
[11] "Gala Opening Week Dedicates New Recital Hall," *Focus.* Fall 1992, 14.
[12] "Win Case Named Men's Head Basketball Coach," *Focus.* Fall 1992," 36.
[13] *Focus.* Fall 1992, 37.
[14] "OCU Arts and Sciences Building Named for President Walker," *Focus.* Fall 1992, 41.
[15] "Soccer to Join Women's Athletic Program," *Focus.* Fall 1993, 32.
[16] "Naming Opportunities Available for New Law Center," *Focus.* Fall 1993, 36.
[17] "Construction projects Address the University's Present Needs, Future Growth," *Focus.* Winter 1993, 2-3.
[18] "Chiefs Capture Third NAIA Crown," *Focus.* Spring 1994, 27.
[19] "Dr. Freda Deskin—The ASTEC Vision," *Focus.* Spring 1997, 25.
[20] "Nursing School Named for Kramers," *Focus.* Winter 1995, 2.
[21] " University Honors Tucker with Naming of Hall," Ibid., 20.
[22] "Petree Legacy Continues," Ibid., 2-3.
[23] 1995. OCU Community Responds to Oklahoma City Disaster. *Focus.* Spring. 21.
[24] 1995. Chiefs Conclude Successful Season at Championships. *Focus.* Spring. 28.
[25] "Bringing Back the Classics" Homecoming 1995. *Focus.* Fall 1995, 1.
[26] "OCU Becomes Largest Private University," Ibid., Fall 1995, 13.
[27] "Writing Across Curriculum Spells Success For Students," Ibid., 28.
[28] "NAIA Champions: Fourth Title in Six Years," Ibid., 2.
[29] " NAIA Champions," *Student Focus.* Summer 1996.
[30] "Leadership: OCU President Jerald Walker Reaches Milestone" *Focus.* Fall, 1996, 9
[31] "New Home for OCU Sororities to Break Ground Fall '97," *Focus.* Spring 1997, 6.
[32] "Roy Clark Performs Benefit Concert," Ibid., 8.
[33] "Dr. Freda Deskin—The ASTEC Vision," Ibid., Spring 1997, 25.
[34] "Dr. Jerald C. Walker—An 18-Year Retrospective," Ibid., Fall 1997, 14-15.
[35] "Cawthon Named Interim President," *Focus.* Fall 1997, 16-17.
[36] "Meinders School Receives Professional Accreditation," Ibid., Fall 1997. 20-21.
[37] "Sports Updates," Ibid., Spring/Summer 1998, 16.
[38] "Dr. Stephen G. Jennings Selected OCU's President," *Focus.* Spring/Summer, 2-3.
[39] "Jennings Inaugurated As 15th President," *Focus.* Summer 1999, 3.
[40] "1999 NAIA National Champions," *Focus.* Summer 1999, 11.

Chapter Ten: A New Century

[1] *Focus Magazine,* spring/summer 2000, p. 4
[2] *Focus Magazine,* spring/summer 2000, p. 5
[3] *Focus Magazine,* spring/summer 2000, p. 6
[4] *Focus Magazine,* spring/summer 2000, p. 8
[5] *Focus Magazine,* spring/summer 2000, p. 14
[6] *Focus Magazine,* fall 2001
[7] *Focus Magazine,* fall 2001, 2.
[8] *Focus Magazine,* winter/spring 2002, 30.
[9] *Focus Magazine,* fall 2002, 15.
[10] *Focus Magazine,* fall 2002, 12.
[11] *Focus Magazine,* fall 2002, 13.
[12] *Focus Magazine,* fall 2002, 14.
[13] *Focus Magazine,* spring 2003, 4.
[14] *Focus Magazine,* spring 2003, 21.
[15] "Redefined," *Constellation,* vol. 00, 2003, 48.
[16] *Oklahoma City University Bulletin,* May 1952.

Index

Index